LILY ALLEN

LILY ALLEN
Living Dangerously

MARTIN HOWDEN

JOHN BLAKE

Published by John Blake Publishing Ltd,
3 Bramber Court, 2 Bramber Road,
London W14 9PB, England

www.blake.co.uk

This paperback edition first published in 2008

ISBN 978 1 84454 631 2

British Library Cataloguing-in-Publication Data:

A catalogue record for this book is available from the British Library.

Design by www.envydesign.co.uk

Printed and bound in Great Britain by Creative Print & Design.
Blaina. Wales.

1 3 5 7 9 10 8 6 4 2

© Text copyright Martin Howden 2008
© Photography WENN

Papers used by ... produced ... The m...

Every attempt has been made ... olders,
but some ... riate

ACKNOWLEDGEMENTS

With thanks to Ian Garland for editing and additional writing, Nia Pejsak (editing and research) and Chloe McCloskey (research).

CONTENTS

CHAPTER ONE

GROWING UP

'They do fuck you up, your mum and dad, but that damage can make you an interesting person.'

Lily Rose Beatrice Allen was born on 2 May 1985. There is something quite prophetic in the timing: the year she was born was declared International Youth Year by the United Nations. Elsewhere Ronald Reagan was sworn in for his second term as the President of the United States of America, Madonna married hell-raising actor Sean Penn and pop music was doing its bit for charity with the very first Live Aid. On a smaller scale, ska band the Specials disbanded. They would be one of Lily's favourite groups and her music would one day be compared favourably to that of her heroes. It would, however, be a long time before the baton was passed.

Lily's upbringing was not a normal one. It was to be a childhood spent competing with a medley of larger-than-life characters. Her older sister Sarah was to be a wayward teenager always in trouble; her younger brother Alfie would suffer from attention deficit disorder; and there would be a number of half-brothers and sisters playing a supporting role in her life story.

Her mother was Alison Owen, a punk fanatic with aspirations of a career as a film producer. Her father was Keith Allen. A larger-than-life personality, Keith was a little bit actor, a little bit comedian, a little bit unlikely pop star and a lot drunk. Both were free spirits who brought Lily into a bohemian world frequented by rockers new and old; upstart artists and Hollywood royalty including the Clash frontman Joe Strummer, Happy Mondays dancer Bez, controversial artist Damien Hirst and actress Gwyneth Paltrow.

Keith and Alison married in 1983. Alison was his first wife, but it wasn't the first time he had started a family. He already had a son called Kevin and daughters Sarah and Grace from previous relationships, while daughters Galoushka and Teddie were to follow. All of them bar Alfie and Lily would have different mothers.

It might be hard to believe nowadays, but Lily was a quiet child. There would come a time when her loud-mouthed opinions would be an almost daily source of amusement to anyone reading her blogs or the morning newspapers, but growing up as a middle child in a boisterous family meant that, rather than compete for the spoils in the household drama, Lily preferred to be out of sight, out of mind.

Lily was wary of causing a fuss and would instead spend hours at a time observing her dysfunctional family in such minute detail and stillness they would often forget she was even there. 'Until I was 12 I had this blanket that I would hold and suck my thumb. And for ages I wouldn't say a word. I was so quiet I think people forgot I was there in a way. I'd just sit and watch what everyone was doing – observing them and their conversations,' Lily recalls.

And there would be plenty to observe during her childhood. She would live primarily in London, although there would be a short stay in Ireland and regular trips abroad with her working parents. But London was to be her home, and it would take on a number of guises. Throughout her childhood she would live in Hammersmith, Shepherd's Bush and Bloomsbury before moving to a luxury, four-storey Victorian house in Islington, north London – which can be seen briefly at the beginning of her music video 'LDN'.

The locations may have constantly changed but there would be one absolute. Whenever there was excitement it would be accompanied by a familiar sight – a young girl sucking her thumb, with a piercing, focused gaze intensely taking everything in around her. Beside her she held a treasured item tightly as if in fear she would lose it. For some this might have looked like a raggy cloth; for Lily it was her precious comfort blanket.

With her vantage viewpoint she would witness family dramas, boisterous evening gatherings and the stillness of her home when her parents were away working. Mistaking silence for contentment, and mindful of the constant attention Alfie and Sarah needed, Lily's parents unsurprisingly left her to her own devices.

Her famous father would be surrounded by people giving him all the attention ('I'd be like, "Hello! Over here!"' she remembers) while her mother was busy working to support them. 'I did probably lack a bit of the tender loving care that most kids get if their mum's at home all the time,' she says. 'I suppose all I really wanted was someone to put their arms around me and give me a big hug, and that never really came. It's not that my mum didn't love us, though – she loves us lots. But she was working incredibly hard to get a roof over our heads.'

Lily wasn't to know it but her ability to observe with a keen but understated eye would play a major part when she started to think seriously about being a pop star.

When Lily was four her parents split up, divorcing soon after. It was to prove a major turning point in her life, and one that still rankles with her today – at least when faced with accusations of an easy life because of her famous dad and her mother, who would receive an Oscar nomination as producer of the 1998 film *Elizabeth*.

'My mother came to London when she was 17 years old with one daughter and a suitcase and nothing else – no money, no education. She was a punk. And we didn't have any money for the first ten years of my life.'

Lily would spend the following years, after her parents split, without Keith, watching her mother fraught with worry as she tried to juggle her career as well as raising her handful of a family. Lily would recall living on a council estate, with money always in short supply.

'My mum came from that background, but she just worked really hard to feed us and keep a roof over our head, and that probably keeps my eyes open. But people don't see that because now my mum is a film producer and my dad is an actor. And they think it must be really easy – "she was really rich" – and that's not true.

'I spent the first nine years of my life in a council flat eating spaghetti on toast. My mum would be on the phone begging my dad for money. So, yeah, my mum knew Anthony Minghella. We'd sit there at a premiere with Gwyneth Paltrow. Mum would get paid to do one job, but it had to last a long time: mortgage, tax and three kids' school fees.

'My dad left home when I was four. I didn't speak to him really until I was 15.'

This telling comment is both half-true and 100 per cent accurate. Although she did see her father on many occasions while growing up, communicating with his daughter was not one of Keith's strongest points. He would take her to football matches to see his beloved Fulham FC play. Lily remembers, 'The only way that my father could communicate with me was by pretending I was his son, taking me to the football, wrapping a scarf around me and patting me on the head.'

However, he was affectionate to Alfie and Lily. And he still speaks to them almost daily and begins and ends every call with 'I love you, love, love you.'

In 1997 Keith made a documentary for Channel Four about his experiences with education. But it was when he went home to film a sequence with his own father that the real story emerged. *Travels with My Camera* was a painful portrayal of a son trying to communicate with his emotionally distant father.

'You can't make your parents be more emotional. You can't hold them guilty for that. My grandfather never touched or held my father. He was very much a victim of his time. Parents of that generation just didn't ever say such things. So now I'm always hugging my children, and saying "I love you."'

At seven Lily and her family moved in with her mother's new boyfriend, British comedian Harry Enfield – who is best known for his comic characters Kevin the Teenager and Smashie and Nicey.

Keith, who knew Enfield, was surprisingly comfortable about the whole situation: 'Of course I still speak to Harry. I never had a problem with it.'

Lily's family had a major impact on Enfield's life. In

an interview in 1995 he admitted Alison and her children had 'made a new man out of me'.

He said, 'Before it was just me – now it's we. With these four people in my life I could only grow. I suddenly feel anything is possible. I just think Alison, Sarah, Lily and Alf are rather nice to put up with me, so I couldn't be nasty to them – they might get up and go.' These were prophetic words as Alison split up with Harry within a few months of the interview after almost three years together.

It was another major setback for Lily. A family friend told the *Sun* newspaper that Lily liked Harry. 'Harry and Alison were going to tie the knot and he was very fond of her three kids, but it all fell apart.'

Lily has never spoken publicly about that period of her life. But it couldn't have been an easy one. 'My mum was in and out of rehab. I never used to see my dad. My mum was so out of her head half the time that she'd forget I was there.'

But Lily was showing remarkable signs of becoming a girl light years ahead of others her age. By the mid-nineties, Alison, despite her personal setbacks, was starting to forge a career as a successful film producer. She noticed her daughter's precocious nature and felt it would be good for her self-esteem to let her mingle with her socialite friends, who instantly warmed to this inquisitive little girl.

At glitzy dinner parties Lily soon developed an easy knack for charming her mum's friends. She shrugged off her childhood shyness and developed a fiendish appetite for questions – most of them directed at authority. 'My mum took me to dinner parties, because I was the one she could do that with. I was really pretentious and precocious. People would say things, and I'd be like, "That's really difficult, how did that make you feel?" and they'd be like, "Fuck off, you're only ten!"'

She was growing at a breathless pace and took with ease to the world of socialising and late-night dinner parties, where she wowed the adults with her grown-up talk. She revelled in this new role. Suddenly she had found a voice that could be heard over those of her louder siblings. She was no longer the middle child, the quiet one or the one hiding behind her comfort blanket. She was overshadowing her family members by being herself. All at once she had become her own person.

At the age of 11 Lily was spotted by a woman who noticed something in her she had noticed only once before. The woman was one of rock music's most notorious ladies – Courtney Love, lead singer of the rock band Hole, but better known for her marriage to the late Nirvana star Kurt Cobain.

Love was shocked when she saw this little wallflower playing grown-up at London's Groucho Club, one of Keith Allen's famed haunts. She was enamoured with the young Lily and fascinated by how well-spoken and worldly-wise this child was.

It wasn't long before she realised that Lily bore an uncanny resemblance to one of her closet friends, Drew Barrymore. After becoming an American sweetheart at the age of seven in the 1982 film *E.T.*, Barrymore fell off the rails as a teenager and succumbed to the temptations Hollywood offers to the young and famous. She was a regular at glitzy showbiz parties with her mother Jaid.

But Courtney saw beyond the headlines when she looked at her friend and realised that Drew in her youth was just a sweet, precocious girl longing for the day when she could finally be an adult. That was something Courtney immediately saw in Lily. She recalled that first encounter with the young girl: 'She wasn't bratty at all, she was like a really nice kid. I remember like I remember Drew before I was friends with her – it's not like she had big boobs or anything early, but she was sort of like 40 when she was 11, and a really sweet little girl.'

For Lily, though, it was a bittersweet compliment.
On the one hand here was someone much older than
her realising correctly what she was going through: 'I
remember being young and thinking, I just want to
be old so that everyone listens to me and takes me
seriously,' she says. On the other hand it was her first
stab at being an individual and she was already being
overshadowed and compared to someone else. This
was to be a theme that dominated Lily's childhood.

CHAPTER TWO

LILY'S DADDY

'The "Wildman of comedy" sounds better than the "Wildman of character acting".' KEITH ALLEN

When Lily Allen first appeared on the scene, she was 'Keith Allen's singer daughter', and for good reason. Keith had been around for decades, quietly carving out a very successful career in movies, TV and music.

He has never been a superstar, but his CV shows that Keith has worked with some of the biggest names in film over the past 25 years and held down key roles in some of the brightest TV shows. Keith was working as a comedian and appearing in small roles in TV shows and British films when he hooked up with the *Comic Strip* gang and his screen career began to take off. He appeared in 17 episodes of the show, alongside such household names of British comedy as Dawn French, Jennifer Saunders, Rik Mayall and Adrian Edmondson.

In the early 1990s he landed movie roles, playing alongside Harvey Keitel in *The Young Americans* – produced by ex-wife Alison – taking the pivotal role of the corpse in British cult classic *Shallow Grave*, and a year later starring alongside Ewan McGregor and Catherine Zeta-Jones in the surfing movie *Blue Juice*.

It seemed that when British movies were being made or Hollywood movies were being shot in Britain, Keith was the first to know, and the first name on the cast list. In 1996 he landed a role alongside Ted Danson and Joely Richardson in *Loch Ness*. The theme continued, with Keith appearing in Brit flicks *Trainspotting*, *Twin Town*, *Rancid Aluminium* and *24 Hour Party People*.

In 2001 he popped up again in a surprise role, as a spooky manservant in the Nicole Kidman movie *The Others*, and even played composer Irving Berlin in the Kevin Kline and Ashley Judd musical *De-Lovely*.

Keith was one of the busiest and most successful character actors in Britain. If it was a surprise to those who knew him only from his drunken exploits in the tabloids, it wasn't to those who continually cast him. Keith was talented and versatile and able to switch comfortably between drama and comedy. For proof of this, see his appearances in the highly acclaimed TV comedy classics *Spaced* and *Black Books* and his regular role in TV show *Bodies*, on the set of which he met his current partner, Tamzin Malleson, who gave birth to his eighth child, daughter Teddie, in 2006.

Rather than seek superstardom, Keith had always been content playing important but primarily character roles, letting other stars take the limelight. It was bizarre for him to see his young daughter's fame suddenly eclipse his – but Keith had a role up his sleeve that he joked would turn the tables again.

In 1995 he was cast as baddie the Sheriff of Nottingham in a new, big-budget production of *Robin Hood* for the BBC. Keith said of the role: 'He does a lot of ranting and shouting but he's a master plotter as well. He's sort of obsessive-compulsive but he's also very funny, in a sly way. He is strangely asexual. His wife ran off with a Norman conqueror and he's never got over it. But if he did feel frisky he'd probably go for a boy – or a goat.'

The swashbuckling series was shot on location in Budapest and filming was both dramatic and painful for Keith – it took him away from his new family and left him aching all over. He was filming in the Hungarian capital when his daughter Teddie was born and he had to stay in touch via webcam. 'I hate being away,' he said at the time. 'I miss everything about home actually – although Budapest is a wonderful place.'

He also needed medical attention twice after accidents on the set – first when he came off his galloping horse. He recalled: 'I got thrown off quite badly. Actually the stuntmen applauded because I fell brilliantly. The horse went one way, I went the other and I ruptured my groin. The whole area was bruised, in fact my cock went black. People couldn't believe it when I showed them! Now I just do a bit of trotting, but that's it – the stuntmen do all the galloping.'

He then lost a tooth when he was elbowed in the mouth during a fight scene. 'Luckily Hungary is the dentistry capital of the world. I quite like having a removable tooth – that way I've got the choice. It will be brilliant if I ever play a pirate.'

After impressing as the dastardly Sheriff of Nottingham, Keith was signed up to star in the 2007 film *The Good Night*, about a former pop star who suffers a midlife crisis. The film stars Penelope Cruz, Danny DeVito, Martin Freeman, Michael Gambon and Keith's ex-wife Alison's pal Gwyneth Paltrow, and is directed by Paltrow's brother Jake.

Keith has enjoyed a long and successful career working alongside his brother Kevin, who is nine years his junior. Despite the age difference, the pair started acting around the same time, and they have used any opportunity to team up on screen. They first appeared together in early episodes of *The Comic Strip Presents…*

In the 1990s the pair teamed up for two cult British films, appearing together in *Trainspotting* and again in 1997's *Twin Town*, which was set in their native Swansea and was written and directed by Kevin. The film earned Kevin a nomination for the Golden Bear at the Berlin International Film Festival.

Kevin followed that two years later with *The Big Tease*, which starred Craig Ferguson – now a successful US talk-show host – as a flamboyant hairdresser. It wasn't a huge success, but it helped Kevin into the director's chair for the 2004 big-budget sequel *Agent Cody Banks 2: Destination London*, starring Frankie Muniz, Anthony Anderson and some familiar faces – Keith Allen, Alfie Owen-Allen and Damien Hirst!

Keith claims he has never been given the recognition for his acting that he deserves – because of his reputation as a party animal. He once claimed: 'I'm good. Bloody good. The best,' and insisted he was unfairly tagged, because: 'The "Wildman of comedy" sounds better than the "Wildman of character acting".'

He went on to say: 'Television is awful. I loathe it, although it must be a godsend for people who don't like social interaction. I do it because I'm good and for the money.'

Despite an acting CV that stretches longer than both his arms, Keith is as famous for his forays into music as he is for his small- and big-screen successes.

After helping to write New Order's 1990 World Cup song 'World In Motion', Keith was angry to be overlooked the next time England qualified for the tournament in 1998. Instead, 'England United', a collaboration between the Spice Girls, Ocean Colour Scene's Simon Fowler and Echo and the Bunnymen was chosen: '(How Does It Feel To Be) On Top Of The World'.

In protest, Keith got together with artist pal

Damien Hirst and Blur bassist Alex James and formed the band Fat Les. They recorded 'Vindaloo', a sing-a-long ode to all things English. Keith wrote the song in a limo on the way back from watching Fulham triumph. 'It was my 44th birthday,' he said, 'and I had hired the car with Alex James from Blur to see the game. I wrote it about all the things in life that are peculiarly English. Putting the kettle on, that's a national pastime. Waterloo and Cheddar cheese and knitting – and going out for an Indian! I was going to call it "Chicken Tikka Masala" but I couldn't find a rhyme so I settled on "Vindaloo".'

The trio launched an aggressive promotional campaign and took the song around the country, performing at festivals and on TV shows. Keith was convinced his anthem would trump 'England United'. He boasted at the time: 'We are going to be No. 1. We have had 380,000 pre-orders. That's more than the Spice Girls.'

And he wasn't averse to slagging off the opposition, saying of Echo and the Bunnymen's Ian McCulloch: 'The sad thing about Ian is that he has lost all his credibility, and that's all he ever had.'

He was right. Sort of. 'Vindaloo' beat 'England United', entering the singles chart at No. 2 in June

1998, a week after '(How Does it Feel To Be) On Top Of The World' only made it to No. 9. But both singles missed out on the top spot because of a re-release of Frank Skinner, David Baddiel and the Lightning Seeds' 1996 hit 'Three Lions'. This held 'Vindaloo' off the top position for three weeks, before the two singles fell to fourth and fifth place respectively. 'England United', meanwhile, had disappeared without trace.

Keith wasn't too disappointed – and two years later Fat Les returned, renamed Fat Les 2000, to record a reworded version of the William Blake poem 'Jerusalem', to coincide with England's appearance at the 2000 European Championships in the Netherlands and Belgium. The song performed better than the team – who failed to progress from the group stages – peaking at No. 10 in June and unable to challenge Sonique's 'It Feels So Good' at the top of the charts.

Fat Les had planned to make another song to support the England team at 2006's World Cup in Germany, but when Lily's career began to take off Keith vetoed the idea, fearful he'd overshadow her.

But he intends to return to the studio in time for the 2008 European Championships in Austria and Switzerland. He says, 'There's a whole generation of eight-year-olds ready for it. Football music is the last genuine folk music. Matches are the only time I can think of that you get people singing together spontaneously. Trying to make it clever, or work in the disco, is wrong.'

CHAPTER THREE

LILY'S MUMMY

'My mum would be on the phone begging my dad for money.'

Alison Owen was educated at University College London, but it masked her true aspiration. She wanted to be a punk rocker. When she realised it was a failing dream, she began pursing a career in film production, distribution and development. She started out making pop videos and TV commercials before graduating to TV series and documentaries. Her first success came with the 1991 UK series *Teenage Health Freak*, starring Tony Robinson. The show won the Royal Television Society Award for Best Youth Programme. She followed that up with *Smashie and Nicey – The End of an Era*, which scooped the Silver Rose at the Montreux Festival in Switzerland and was nominated for a BAFTA Award.

It was an impressive start, and one which would lead the all the way to Hollywood. Her first film, *Hear My Song*, which she produced in 1991, was nominated for Golden Globe and BAFTA Awards and won Best Comedy Film at the British Comedy Awards. The Producers Guild of America nominated her as Most Promising New Producer.

Alison had made a mark in the movie world remarkably quickly. She was soon snapped up by British movie house Working Title, where she established a low-budget film division. She returned to producing in 1993 with *The Young Americans*, which starred Harvey Keitel, Viggo Mortensen, a young Thandie Newton in one of her first-ever roles and a certain Keith Allen as a violent London gangster. It was the first time she and Keith worked together – some four years after they divorced!

Alison's career went from strength to strength as she developed a name for herself as a talented and ambitious producer. Her projects became increasingly high-profile and the cast lists more impressive. Her 1994 production *Smashie and Nicey – The End of an Era* was written by and starred her then boyfriend Harry Enfield with co-writer and star Paul Whitehouse.

Her next film, *Moonlight and Valentino*, boasted a cast list including Whoopi Goldberg, Kathleen Turner, Jon Bon Jovi and a starlet who would go on to play a very important role in Alison's career and personal life – Gwyneth Paltrow. It was filmed in Toronto and Alison took Lily to stay with her while she worked on the film. Some of Lily's childhood memories are of getting 'very scared' at the top of the CN Tower, watching the Blue Jays baseball team and being fascinated by 'a big building with Domino's Pizza on it'.

Alison and Gwyneth wouldn't reunite on a movie set for the best part of a decade – by which time Paltrow was Hollywood's hottest leading lady and Owen was a major movie industry player.

In 1998 Alison made the movie that established her name in Hollywood, *Elizabeth*. Starring Cate Blanchett as the Virgin Queen, it had an incredible ensemble cast including Sir Richard Attenborough, Sir John Gielgud, Geoffrey Rush, Vincent Cassel, Emily Mortimer, Christopher Eccleston, Kathy Burke and Kelly Macdonald. There was even room for cameo roles for an 11-year-old Alfie Owen-Allen and 13-year-old Lily Allen as a lady-in-waiting. The film earned six Academy Award nominations, including one for Alison in the Best Picture category. She missed out to *Shakespeare in Love*, *Elizabeth* only picking up the Best Make-Up award.

Alison later reminisced about her Academy Award experience: 'On the day the nominations came out, I was having lunch with my sister. Afterwards, I was walking up Oxford Street and my fellow producer Eric Fellner was scanning the street, looking for me. He said, "We've been nominated." I said, "What for?" The Oscars just weren't on our radar.

'After that, it all got rather stupid. I had designers ringing me up to offer me dresses to wear. Harry Winston gave me diamonds. Then there was that whole rollercoaster machine of publicity people and stylists trying to get the most out of you. Polygram – they hired publicity people and placed adverts – handled the actual award campaign but it was all done out in LA; I didn't know what was going on.

'The strangest thing about Oscar night is the place-sitters at the theatre. You only have to get up from your seat for a second and someone in a pink dress promptly hops into it. It sounds silly, but it creates a real problem: you come back from the bar and see someone in your seat and naturally assume that you can't sit back down. It was very disorientating.'

The film was nominated for twelve BAFTA Awards, and won five, including the Alexander Korda Award for Best British Film for Alison.

The accolades confirmed Alison's status in the Hollywood system. Her next big job would reunite her with Keith. The TV movie *Is Harry on the Boat?*, about a group of booze- and sex-obsessed holiday reps, was a rare venture away from feature films, and she was soon back doing what she loved most – making movies.

Next up was the horror movie *Happy Now*, starring Ioan Gruffud and Jonathan Rhys Meyers. In 2003 Alison was reunited with Gwyneth Paltrow, who had gone from fresh-faced young starlet to Oscar-winning, multi-million-dollar-commanding mega star – in fact she lifted her Best Actress Oscar for *Shakespeare in Love*, in 1999, the same year Alison missed out on one.

Eight years after they had worked together on *Moonlight and Valentino*, Alison cast Gwyneth in the lead role in *Sylvia*, about writer and poet Sylvia Plath and her poet husband Ted Hughes.

Sylvia was a long-term dream of Alison's and she fought tooth and nail to overcome the pessimism of

Hollywood bigwigs, who were worried about making a film that ends in suicide (Sylvia's). She succeeded and future James Bond star Daniel Craig was cast as Hughes opposite Paltrow's Plath.

The pair followed that collaboration two years later with *Proof*, which Alison produced and Gwyneth starred in as the daughter of Anthony Hopkins's brilliant mathematician. By this time the pair were colleagues and business partners, forming GoGo Pictures together. And they were close friends too. Alison was around in 2003 to help Gwyneth cope with her grief following the death of her dad, director Bruce Paltrow, in October 2002.

Alison later said of their friendship: 'I could see when Gwyneth was feeling a bit down and I was able to reach out and squeeze her hand or go and have a little cry with her.' She claimed their friendship was so strong because Paltrow was 'The same girl she was when I first met her. Gwyneth makes judgments about someone very quickly, very instinctively and decides whether she likes or dislikes them. She's very instinctive about who she places her trust in, and once she makes up her mind, it's difficult for her to change it.'

Speaking in 2003 about Paltrow's relationship with Coldplay frontman Chris Martin – whom she married in December 2003 – Alison added: 'She's in a very good place right now. Everything is coming together. She's very happy in her personal life.'

As well as her collaboration with Paltrow, Alison was also the co-founder of Ruby Films, with Neris Thomas. The company produced her films *Bait*, *Rat*, *Is Harry on the Boat?*, *Happy Now*, *Sylvia* and *Love +Hate*, as well as *Love and Other Disasters* and *Brick Lane*.

Collaborations have been an important part of Alison's career, and she has regularly gone back to work again with writers and producers, actors and actresses she has got on well with. She first worked with respected New Zealand filmmaker Tim Bevan on *Moonlight and Valentino* in 1995 and their friendship endured with a further collaboration on *Elizabeth* and *Rachel's Holiday*, scheduled for release in 2008. Alison returned the favour by helping Bevan produce the 2004 horror/comedy *Shaun of the Dead*, which was written by and starred *Spaced* star Simon Pegg.

Life as a big-shot producer hasn't been all smooth for Alison, however. In 2004 she had to scrap the £45-million film *Tulip Fever*, based on Deborah Moggach's novel, because of a change in UK tax laws. She had been developing the project for six years, had recruited a director, John Madden, and Tom Stoppard had written the screenplay – the pair had collaborated on *Shakespeare in Love*. Jude Law, Keira Knightley and Jim Broadbent were lined up to star – but the plug was pulled at the last minute.

'I am no expert on tax; I'm a film producer,' Alison said at the time. 'I read books and think about which ones would make a good movie, and then I work with directors in order to make them. I bought the rights to the book *Tulip Fever*. We had one final conference call with all the backers booked, just to dot the i's and cross the t's on the final points of the agreement. I got a call from DreamWorks telling me that a change in the tax laws had been put through that effectively removed 30 per cent of our funding.

'My understanding is that the previous system was set up to enable people to invest in films in the UK and set that against tax losses, but now they're not allowed to do that any more.

'Anything that was signed was OK, but anything that was not signed was not OK. If they had announced it on Wednesday rather than Tuesday, we would have been OK. Instead it has been catastrophic.

'We had already incurred $6 million worth of

spending, so our film has collapsed, and there's no possibility of saving it. Absolutely none.

'I've written to Gordon Brown and the Paymaster General, Dawn Primarolo. Tom Stoppard has spoken to Steven Spielberg about it, and I believe he has called Tony Blair. I've been in close contact with the British Film Council and all the other people who are lobbying on our behalf. If nothing changes, I'm going to have to dismantle the whole project. We've got everyone working on a week's notice. So if I can't rehire people tomorrow then I'm going to have to let them go.

'It's all surreal, to be honest. I feel dreadfully sorry for the 80 people I'll have to give notice to on Friday. My company will probably fold, because I haven't been paid a penny yet for those six years' work. We were only due to receive money when the film went into shooting. I'm going to get nothing for six years' work. And I now owe DreamWorks $6 million.'

The film was dismantled – but Alison wasn't defeated and her career continues to flourish with the films *The Other Boleyn Girl*, starring Natalie Portman, Scarlett Johansson, Eric Bana and Kristin Scott-Thomas, *Brideshead Revisited* and *Rachel's Holiday*, an adaptation of the Marian Keyes novel which is expected to star Catherine Zeta-Jones.

CHAPTER FOUR

LIVING IN THE SHADOWS

'I'm the biggest show-off in the world.'
Keith Allen

It was the summer of 1998 and the era of Brit Pop was in full swing – an era when the alpha male was king. Oasis were the biggest guitar band since the Beatles, lads' magazines with countless pages of scantily clad women were being snapped up off the shelves, male fashion consisted primarily of combed-down hair and Ben Sherman shirts worn outside the trousers and the England football team were attempting to win their first World Cup since 1966. The atmosphere was perfect for Keith to display a trait his daughter Lily would later pick up on and copy – his love of sticking two fingers up at the establishment.

England United – comprising the Spice Girls, Ocean Colour Scene's Simon Fowler and Echo and the Bunnymen – were providing the official World Cup anthem, '(How Does it Feel To Be) On Top Of The World'. Keith – who had played a part in the 1990 World Cup anthem by co-writing the New Order song 'World In Motion' – saw his chance to be the people's hero, a chance to give real football fans the terrace chant they had always wanted.

The song was 'Vindaloo'. It captured the buzz in the British air perfectly, reaching No. 2 in the UK, and was easily more memorable than the official anthem, which lasted just three weeks in the Top Forty and barely scraped into the Top Ten.

After a successful recording on *Top of the Pops*, the BBC chart show had its own outdoor party to celebrate. It was a raucous affair, as any party with Keith on the guest list would be. Beer and wine flowed, voices were raised and spirits were high. In the middle of it all, someone noticed a small 13-year-old girl with cropped dark hair and grungy clothes swaggering through the crowd with inbuilt charisma. She sat down by herself and started to take a drink of the vodka and tonic in her hand. She gazed wearily at her father, who was surrounded by a group of people she didn't recognise.

As usual he was excitedly telling another one of his anecdotes – could it be the one where his friend Damien Hirst once put a penis on a plate and handed it to actor Stephen Fry with the question 'Sausage, sir?' to which Fry didn't even bat an eyelid. Or maybe it was about the black cab he owned for a laugh and had insured so a vagrant called Outside Dave could drive him around London when he got too drunk. Whatever the story – and there were a lot –he was the centre of attention.

The young girl rolled her eyes and took another sip of vodka and tonic. Her name was Lily Allen. One guest asked her, 'Does your dad know you're drinking?' Lily, nodding to her father, replied, 'With his track record he could hardly complain, could he?'

The guest left Lily by herself but kept an eye on the young girl to see what retribution, if any, would come once her father realised she was drinking alcohol. It would be a long wait. As the party goer recalled, 'Keith didn't once come over to Lily and say: "What the hell are you doing?" He couldn't really, because he was just a few feet away getting pretty drunk himself, yet she was the youngest person there by a mile.'

It was not the first time Keith was spotted with his kids drinking while they were under age. That same year at the Glastonbury music festival, he was wheeling a karaoke machine around when he saw Alfie, his 12-year-old son. Alfie was looking the worse for wear when his dad demanded: 'Have you been fucking drinking?' Keith then smirked, with a twinge of pride: 'You little fucker.'

But Keith had a method to his parenting. In an interview in 2002 he revealed, 'I don't hide anything with my kids, we are really close. We talk about everything together. I give them lots of lectures – just as every parent does. In my view you have to accept that children will experiment with drugs and drink.

'It is bad but there is no getting away from that. I think it is important to educate kids and help them make informed decisions. They need to know the consequences of what will happen if they do get drunk or take drugs.

'I have a ridiculous rule. I won't let my daughter smoke in front of me. I know she does and I know it is stupid, but at least there is some tiny bit of order. I used to love rules because then I could break them.' Like father, like daughter.

Lily saw his and Alison's parenting methods differently, though. 'I did grow up in a very liberal family and I was able to pretty much do whatever I wanted, in the sense of I wasn't very well disciplined.'

As guests remember it, at the *Top of the Pops* party Lily was drinking but she was not misbehaving. The reveller said, 'She was a sweet girl, but seemed much older than her years. She was very full-on and confident – precocious like one of those stage-school kids – but absolutely tiny. You could tell she felt comfortable in the world her father inhabited and very much wanted to be a part of it.'

You could also say that sometimes it was hard to spot which one was the parent, which one was the kid. It didn't feel like Keith wanted to grow up. His childish possessions include a gypsy houseboat and the aforementioned black cab.

Keith was very much associated with the rise of the lad culture in the 1990s, with his wide-boy antics making him a very willing elder statesman of the movement.

Keith believed his own children accepted him in the same way. As he said in an interview in 2002, 'Incredibly, kids find Fat Les cool so my kids never get any hassle at school. They don't have any hang-ups about me being famous, thank God.'

But he had got it wrong on a number of counts. First of all, Lily didn't like Fat Les, even going as far as to admit she 'cringes' when she sees the 'Vindaloo' video. More importantly she did mind her father being famous, primarily because it kept him away from her, but also because it meant no matter what she did, people would compare her with her famous father. Here was a strong-willed girl growing up with a constant battle for her identity.

It didn't help that she had not settled on the career she wanted. But she did want to be famous. Not because of the glamour or the riches – being famous meant having your own voice, it meant that you could be your own person and it also meant that, for once, she could live her life with no responsibility for anyone but herself, something she craved more than anything.

'When I was really, really young, I visited my dad on a film set. We stayed in a trailer, and every morning someone would come and get him up and put him in a car so he could go off and do what he had to do. I remember thinking, That's great, I want to be famous,' she recalled.

Fortunately, being the offspring of a famous personality does have its benefits. The late Clash star Joe Strummer was a close friend of Keith, and the rocker would play a big, if an unwitting, part in Lily's career as musician. No one knew it at that stage but 'Uncle Joe', as Lily called him, was introducing her to an eclectic collection of punk, ska and reggae records. Growing up, she never really understood why everyone loved Joe and stopped him on the street to speak to him.

'I didn't know Joe Strummer was from a really famous rock band until the day he died [in 2002]. I just always thought of him as Uncle Joe, my dad's best friend, and I probably spent two days of every month with him since the day I was born. It was only when I went to his funeral that I was like "What the...? Uncle Joe was a famous rocker" and I had no idea.'

Lily was also soon diving into her mother's vast record collection and excitedly soaking up a wide range of music – not that Keith had any inkling his daughter had musical aspirations. In an interview with the *Daily Mirror* at the start of the millennium he claimed, 'Lily's got a good voice. She doesn't want to go into showbiz. She is very introverted but is a natural. She really likes her dad. I can get her into nightclubs and I can get her tickets to Glastonbury.'

For the 2002 World Cup Fat Les brought out a song called 'Who Invented Fish and Chips?' Alfie got a part in the video for the song. 'I think it's great that people come up and ask where the new Fat Les World Cup song is,' said Keith. 'It's like a pension plan – which is really daft, as you don't make any money out of it. I always put my kids in the video. My son and his mates are in the background and we called them the No Salad Crew.'

For a song that was much derided it almost doesn't deserve its place in music history. But it was Lily's professional singing debut.

Cameos in her dad's novelty band aside, Lily had no idea what she wanted to do. She was trying several guises on for size to see how they fitted. When she enquired about acting, her mum got her a walk-on part in her latest film, *Elizabeth*. Appearing as part of a background may have been Lily's thing when she was a tot but was not what she needed now. Standing with a group of other extras, who were only there to supply a moving backdrop while her mother fussed with the bigger stars of the picture, didn't – unsurprisingly – sit well with Lily's sudden need to be centre of attention.

She was looking to rebel, but at what? Her father was an actor, a singer, a comedian and a working-class rebel. Her mother was a hard-working former punk rocker reviving the British film industry.

While growing up, Lily shared her disillusionment with her best friend, Miquita Oliver. Miquita would become a star in her own right as presenter on Channel 4 youth show *T4*, but at that time she and Lily were two young pals struggling to find something rebellious that their parents hadn't done more excessively themselves. They would look on in envy when their parents got together, glumly admitting that their parties were far better than their own would ever be.

Miquita, like Lily, was born into 1980s bohemia. Her mother was the Rip, Rig and Panic singer, broadcaster and single mum Andrea Oliver. Again, like Lily's, her parents' house was a bustling Who's Who of Britain of that time. Her aunt was the singer Neneh Cherry, famed stylist Judy Blame was 'like a godfather to us all', Boy George would come round – prompting Miquita to hide in her bathroom because she was 'terrified of him' – while her favourite adult visitor was 'that mental violinist with the spiky hair', Nigel Kennedy.

But it was an overpowering and intimidating atmosphere for both kids and they would dream about 'living an ordinary, boring, suburban childhood in a nice house in Kent'. The two are still friends today, and Miquita is glad her pop star pal makes good music because she would hate to have to pretend she liked it. 'I'm just glad she's made it with a record I like. I listen to it. Though she doesn't know that, obviously.'

Where did it leave Lily?

The essence of rebellion is going against your parents' wishes – yet it seemed Lily's parents were having the time of their lives.

Just before her chart success, Lily approached her father and finally opened up about her resentments. Keith took it on the chin but admits her feelings about him have changed since she has become famous in her own right. 'It's quite interesting, actually, because I've noticed that since she's been famous she's come to realise what it's like to be famous and that it's not as easy as you think. Years ago she would have gone, "Oh, for fuck's sake, you cock" when she read in the papers things that were blatantly not true. But now she's had a bit of that herself and I think it puts it into some kind of context.

'I do read such drivel about me. People want to live their lives by proxy and that just comes with the territory. I'm supposed to be a heroin addict, having an affair with Kate Moss and have held a knife to a commissioning editor's throat.'

The pair are now on very good terms, with Keith phoning her three times a day and making sure she is rehearsing, writing new songs and guiding her through the stress of fame.

He enthused, 'I think one of the really wonderful things about Lily is the way she's dealt with it. She's just taken it in her stride, effortlessly really, which is great, but I think she's come to understand that it's a pretty stormy sea.'

Keith is an understandably proud father, and fears that a celebrated show-off would be somehow jealous of his now more famous daughter are unfounded. Lily wasn't present, but at a recent film premiere Keith was besieged by a group of journalists whose questions were all about his pop-star daughter. Without any hesitation he answered every single one, beaming with pride at every mention of Lily's name.

However, lying there in her bed as a young teenager, listening to Uncle Joe's records and looking out at the street as the world happily passed her by, Lily was not to know that. It would be a long time before she would Google Keith's name and the search result would show 'Lily Allen's father', but it was something she couldn't wait for.

Ever the pessimist, Lily still doesn't take anything

for granted. When she received word that Keith Allen's latest TV show, *Robin Hood*, in which he plays the evil Sheriff of Nottingham, was receiving rave reviews, she ruefully replied, 'I'll be back to being the daughter of Keith Allen tomorrow.'

CHAPTER FIVE

A DRAMATIC
INTERVENTION

'Before she took over the school choir,
I had nothing. All I had was my anger.'
LILY ALLEN ON HER MUSIC TEACHER RACHEL SANTESSO

Despite coming from a family associated with fame, Lily did not want to be a generic pop star. A large part of that is due to the bohemian atmosphere that filtered through her childhood. Although she grew up in a household regularly filled with celebrities, they were not the kind who would turn up in a limousine or display diva-esque behaviour.

They were exuberant types. Drunken anecdotes were passed around the table and there was a ready supply of happy playmates for Lily to be 'chased around the nearby field with'. Uncle Joe would be slumped on the couch with a bottle of whisky in his hand while Damien Hirst and Keith regaled each other with tales of debauchery at the Groucho Club.

Unlike many of her pop peers, there was no dancing around the mirror with a hairbrush in her hand or begging her mum to sign her up for dancing classes. As her father puts it, 'She was never the type to stand under the Christmas tree singing, and thank God, because I'd have walked out of the room.'

Instead, at primary school Lily looked with disdain at her fellow pupils who held those kinds of aspirations. At 11 she was already a disruptive influence, tagged an argumentative problem child. 'I was quite a misguided child,' she admits. 'I think everyone thought I was a bit of a joke. I was very much like my dad, wanting attention, fighting and being very aggressive.'

So she wasn't particularly thrilled about attending music class. While her classmates skipped into the classroom, Lily would shuffle to the back, wipe her unkempt hair away from her face and shy away from everyone else. 'She sat slightly apart from the others in a grouchy little lump. She was a tough little thing, but had these huge, melancholy eyes,' recalls her music teacher, Rachel Santesso.

Despite Lily's brash look and her apparent unwillingness to take part in the class, Santesso had a soft spot for her. One day while walking to her classroom she heard a young voice shyly singing the words to the Oasis song 'Wonderwall'. She turned round to see that the singer was Lily Allen, shuffling her way to another class, blissfully unaware she had this 'sweet, melancholy voice'. Impressed with what she heard, Rachel formulated a plan to get this sensitive side of Lily over to her classmates.

Unaware of what was to come, Lily attended her music class the following day, shoulders slumped as she slouched her way to her seat. The class started as normal, with the kids eager to put on a show. Rachel then called out Lily's name. Her saucer eyes gazed at the young teacher in surprise. She was being called up to sing.

Lily didn't know what to do. 'Why don't you sing that song I heard you sing yesterday? The Oasis song,' Santesso asked. Lily pulled herself up from the desk which she had burrowed herself into and walked to the front of the class, her eyes all the time peering down at the floor. Santesso gently coaxed the young girl into singing the song she had heard sung so beautifully the previous day. Shy at first, but gaining more confidence with each passing second,

Lily transformed herself before her teacher's eyes. Santesso was eager to shower her pupil with compliments. She quickly told Lily's classmates that the troubled little girl was in fact very talented.

After the class had finished and the pupils hurried out of the room, Lily held back a little bit until everyone bar Santesso was left. She shyly went up to her and thanked her for 'saying all those nice things about me'. But for Santesso, praising Lily wasn't about building up her confidence and her low self-esteem, as she genuinely saw talent in her pupil.

'After teaching thousands of students, I can honestly say Lily still stands out as having been an exceptionally talented child. She was a natural musician and singer who also had an enormous talent for words,' she gushed.

That day Lily couldn't have been happier. She started to believe she really could sing. No one had said she had a sweet voice before, and this is the school music teacher so she must know what she is talking about, thought Lily.

She certainly did. Santesso may have been a schoolteacher then, but she would soon forge her own singing career and eventually become an award-winning soprano and composer/arranger who would sing in an audience with Pope John Paul II. But at that time she was just happy to foster the musical development of this special little girl in her class.

When Lily got home she kept singing 'Wonderwall' in her room, trying to relive the moment time and time again.

Despite the young girl's troublesome reputation, Santesso believed that all Lily needed was a stage where she could show off her natural talent. Luckily there was one such show coming up, and one that the majority of the pupils' parents would be attending. Seizing a perfect opportunity for everyone to witness Lily's talent, Santesso approached her and asked her if she would perform. Once Lily said yes, they deliberated over what would be the perfect song for her to showcase her talent.

Despite Lily's best efforts, 'Wonderwall' was not the right song, thought Santesso. She then remembered a song from the Disney film *Dumbo* and quickly tracked it down. And sure enough there was the one line that perfectly summed up Lily at that stage of her life.

'It's the song the mummy elephant sings to the baby elephant,' recalled Lily.

Santesso explained, 'There's a line in it that says how if they knew the sweet little you, then they'd end up loving you. I thought that was appropriate. And it broke my heart every time I heard her sing it.'

She wouldn't be the only one. It promised to be an emotional night. Parents of pupils at the Catholic school gathered in their droves to witness the musical show. Backstage was a whirl of excitement as the kids excitedly got ready to perform their individual numbers.

Lily sat by herself in a corner of the room. She was nervous, understandably so, given the circumstances. This was more than just a little show for mum and dad to film and show relatives. Neither of her parents was there because of their busy workloads and for little Lily this was a chance to show everyone what she was made of.

When her turn came, there was a piercing hush. The girl they had all too easily dismissed as a troublemaker approached the stage cautiously. She glanced around in the hope she would catch a familiar face in the background. There was none to be found.

She started to sing. The response was emphatic. 'They knew me as angry little Lily and everyone just cried, but in a good way. They were like, "Oh my God, she's finally got something,"' recalled Lily.

This unassuming little girl had a voice that touched everyone who was there that night.

Producer Mark Ronson, who would work on Lily's debut album *Alright, Still*, isn't surprised she evoked that kind of response. 'She's very self-deprecating and doesn't realise the gift that she had. I'm always laughing, looking at her in her Nike Air Max 95s and big frock, going, "I can't believe this is the vessel for one of the best pop melody songwriters of a generation."'

Santesso was stunned at what she saw. 'I'll never forget the spell she cast on an audience. Her performance was unforgettable. It was a powerful moment, and I swear to God I knew then, without a doubt, that Lily would be a singer.'

Although it would be a long time before Santesso's prophetic words would come true, it was the start of something special. As Lily mentions in the sleeve notes to *Alright, Still*, it was Santesso who 'found her voice'.

Breathless with excitement, Lily couldn't believe the response. 'My singing had a really good effect on people and I loved that feeling. It was a big turning point for me.'

It was a bittersweet night for Lily, however. She would always remember that 'My mum didn't turn up to the concert, but all the other parents did.'

Santesso is delighted that Lily is following the path

she always believed she was capable of, and gets angry when people claim she only got a record deal because of her parents: 'Those accusations of nepotism are ridiculous. Many people, from Bach to Bjork, had famous parents who were also successful musicians. You either have talent or you don't. And Lily has real, true talent in bucketloads.'

Lily was soon to turn 12. She had decided she was too old for her raggy blanket and got rid of it. For comfort over the years ahead she would need more than a blanket.

CHAPTER SIX
REBELLION AND EXPULSION

'I was definitely the easiest out of my mum's three kids. Well, until I lost my blanket.'

One day, while with their father, Lily and Alfie asked him about his past. They were curious, and had every right to be. Keith's past was a catalogue of drunken encounters and outbursts, jail time, spells in rehab and a steady flow of flings. The media weren't slow to rake everything up. Lily, being the inquisitive one in the family, would read of her dad's exploits with a mixture of a heavy heart and a resigned shrug of the shoulders, muttering 'What's he done now?' like the world-weary mother of a teenage tearaway.

Keith was born on 2 December 1953 in Gorseinon, Swansea, Wales. He was a disruptive and very unsettled child. He was the oldest of three. His father Eddie, a submariner, was posted around the world and would often be gone for long spells. The mantra for Keith while growing up was 'wait till your father comes home'. It would lead to an almost double life for the boy. He knew he was going to get in trouble when his father got back, so in the meantime he would constantly wreak mischief before his dad returned in six months' time. 'I wanted to have some fun,' he recalls.

The cycle would go on until he became too much of a handful. When his father was posted to Singapore he took the whole family, except for Keith, who was promptly sent off to a public school at the age of 11. It was the same age Keith lost his virginity to a 12-year-old on board a disused boat. When asked if he was in a relationship with the young girl, he gasped, 'God, no. Two years later her mother offered herself to me.'

The public school was Brentwood in Essex and he managed to last two years before being expelled for disorderly behaviour. There would be a number of incidents of mischief-making by Keith at Brentwood but the following one shows him at his most disruptive and creative, and is another example of the way he took out his frustrations with authority.

The pupils would regularly attend the school chapel for choir. It was never the most exciting part of the day and one most of them were eager to avoid. Keith, however, thought he could lighten the mood by unscrewing the pipes on the chapel's organ and replacing them in the wrong order. According to Keith, the music master's face when the first hymn started up had to be seen to be believed. Expulsion was the result of that little episode.

Later, while the guest of a detention centre, he gained six O-levels, which earned him entry to the Welsh College of Music and Arts, and he returned to Wales. But once again he ended up expelled, this time for what he claims as 'student union activities': he parked his car in the college principal's parking space and promptly took the wheels off.

Keith was a promising footballer and when playing in the West Wales Youth Clubs final in Swansea he was spotted by a scout. 'I had trials at Southampton and should have had one at Leeds United. But I ended up in Borstal (for cat burglary) instead and missed it. It was really rather stupid. Five of us sneaked into a gig by a band called Spackridge. We climbed over the roof and in through the dressing-room window and saw this coat hanging up with a wallet. I just got there first. It could have been any one of us. So I missed my trial.

'I regret it tremendously. But I would never have made it as a pro. My legs are too short. I played in midfield and I was a nasty piece of work, but I had a good engine. I'm pretty bone idle and if I had made it I would have drunk all my talent away.'

Keith didn't get his anger and mischievousness out of his system at school and college. In 1984, while living with Alison, it would catch up with him again. He spent seven weeks in Pentonville Prison for smashing up London nightclub Zanzibar. 'I have a bit of a chequered past, but I was never a hooligan. Violence has never been my thing. I always liked having a laugh too much and I was a coward. I trashed a nightclub, but that was on my own and nobody got hurt. It's just about property, not people.'

His spell in the detention centre didn't exactly get the desired response: 'Institutions such as jail encourage you to feel like you are a criminal. But I didn't feel like a criminal once. I always thought I was on holiday – just passing through. I enjoyed – it's like, I would be a fool to say that I enjoyed being in Borstal – but when I was there I had a great time.'

It wouldn't be long before Keith would again find

something that would both amuse him and disrupt the workings of the detention centre. 'You had to march under surveillance and I would orchestrate and choreograph a marching pattern so that before we actually marched away I'd say, "Right, every third step move your left leg out." And they used to do it. It was mayhem.'

Coupling memories of all these incidents with accounts of his legendary three-day drinking sessions and the long line of broken relationships and children – including daughter Grace from Linda Peters and Galoushka with Wolverhampton jazz singer Anjel Tabatha – meant the conversation about his past with his two inquisitive children took a while.

He said, 'They know they have a very unconventional dad. "Why were you a thief?" they ask. But at least I can tell them the lessons I have learned. The dialogue is exhausting, but interesting – you learn about yourself in the process. I think they quite like me.'

Lily never had a problem liking her father: in fact she found herself becoming more and more like him every day. She had attended a dozen schools by the time she was 15. She was a disruptive child, and a number of institutions, including Ireland's Scoil

Bhride and Hill House, Millfield, Dunhurst and Bedales in England, bore the brunt of her inherited need to argue against authority and her own low self-esteem. 'I just used to fuck things up for myself,' she admitted.

It was around this time that Lily witnessed a terrible incident. Keith had just got home from a two-day drinking session when he collapsed from an agonising pain in his chest. His horrified cleaner rushed to get help. An ambulance came, followed by his mum and dad, who were nearby. Lily witnessed it all.

This kind of attack wasn't new to Keith. 'The first time it happened to me I thought I was having a heart attack and dying. This time the pain was worse but it was more terrifying for the people around me – I knew what it was. The attacks last about eight hours and you can't lie down, which makes it much worse. The doctors say that it's an oesophageal cardiac spasm caused by a combination of stress and not eating, just drinking.'

Ironically, his ailment makes it impossible to sample the dish that lent its name to Fat Les's debut single. 'It's set off by curries, tomatoes, and I can't even drink a bloody Mary. I can eat a vindaloo but the consequences would be appalling. It's like having severe heartburn, and when it's bad it can last for eight hours. When that happens it is not funny. The symptoms are exactly like those of a heart attack – you can't tell the difference.'

The first time he had a spasm Keith was in such agony he begged his dad to hit him so he would be knocked out. Keith's father managed to contain himself, and instead waited for a nurse, who, recalls Keith, injected 'my backside full of morphine. The doctors ran all these tests and they showed my organs were absolutely brilliant, my heart's fine, my kidneys are fine and my lungs are good. It's encouraging but it made me think I can go out and get more drunk because I've got such a great body!'

It was a near miss for Keith, and it shook Lily up badly.

As a result of her upbringing, Lily found herself able to communicate better with people far older than her, while she found kids of her age too immature. She mixed with the older crowd at school, but that posed new problems. While her friends were allowed to leave school early to prepare for their A-levels, she was left all alone, socially stranded after too long ignoring pupils her age. It would reinforce her longing to become older and have people take her seriously.

A school pal in her year, who did not want to be named, said, 'Lily was a loner at school. She never really seemed to connect with anyone or have any close friends. Us girls all hung around in packs, but she used to spend lots of time on her own. I was really surprised to find out she was a singer. You'd never have known she had it in her. She always seemed so introverted and shy. You'd have thought she'd be singing all the time and humming tunes and fighting to get in school plays and singing in bands at school but there was none of that.'

Academically, Lily was a stubborn pupil. She refused to make any kind of effort with subjects that didn't interest her, saying, 'I'm one of those people that, if I'm not immediately good at something, I give up. I don't like not being brilliant.' It seemed there were very few subjects that did interest her. She would run crying from every exam, she never did her homework and would 'get into fights and drink and smoke and sleep with guys'.

There was one subject she did enjoy – Classical Studies. 'I became obsessed by quite arcane subjects, like Second World War evacuation stories and books about the 18th-century aristocracy. It was just amazing. Greek mythology! I was mesmerised. But it's stories which are fun … I can't remember dates. History: who gives a fuck? So you can sit down at a dinner party in ten years' time and go "Oh, in 1066 the Battle of Hastings … some treaty was signed … or whatever."'

Classical Studies aside, Lily doesn't have many fun memories of school. She puts it down to a lack of stability both at home and at school. 'It was frustrating moving schools so much because I always felt I couldn't articulate my feelings as much as I wanted to. I was very lonely as a kid. I went to so many different schools so never had time to make enduring friendships.'

The schools she was sent to were just not for Lily. Prince Charles's former London prep school, Hill House, was too rigid; she was only sent to Millfield because she was good at hockey and her parents thought the boarding school would be a good restraining influence on her (ironic really, when you consider it was the same reasons young Keith was given by his parents – and look how well that turned out) and she was even too rebellious for the exclusive yet bohemian boarding school Bedales and its junior school Dunhurst.

Lily was still struggling to find herself and, as a result, she was a handful. 'I was officially expelled from two schools and asked to leave by three. It was pretty much for illegal goings on. I just had more important things to worry about.'

She puts it down to teenage arrogance. 'It's why I never succeeded at school. I just hate being told what to do. I'm an incredibly stubborn person, and I don't want to get out of bed for anyone. That's incredibly arrogant.'

On what was to be her last day of school, at 15 years of age, Lily wore a T-shirt with the words 'I am a naughty girl, I am a naughty girl' emblazoned on it. It wasn't long before she was summoned to the headmistress and both thought it would be best for all concerned if Lily left. 'I gave that T-shirt to someone else and she got expelled as well,' she recalled.

Looking back at her school years, Lily realises her chaotic childhood took its toll on her. She would look on her schoolfriends who did their homework without disturbance and on time with awe and jealously. 'I had quite a turbulent upbringing. I was middle-class and everything was quite comfortable, but everyone was mental. I used to be really envious of those kids who could do their homework and bring it in on time and were organised.'

She longed for stability at home, even if it was just a meal with everyone around the table while her mum cooked Lily's favourite dinner – a roast with bread sauce. But it wasn't to be that way. Instead, her family would usually sit around 'the telly with their plate on their knees'.

'Things were fucked up: my mum was having a nervous breakdown, and my dad was doing whatever he was doing in the Groucho. I don't see it like it was anything special, because it was all I knew.'

That was all to change in one pivotal moment – when she started a relationship with a boy called Lester Lloyd. They had met first met when she seven and living in Leixlip, County Kildare, Ireland, for a year while her mother filmed *Hear My Song* there. She had become pals with a young girl called Poppy Lloyd who introduced her to her brother Lester. They got together at 15 after meeting again in London, something Lily describes as a 'mad coincidence'.

Lester decided to take Lily back to meet his parents in Ireland and she was amazed at what she saw. His family was a loving one and evening meals were hearty, homely affairs with laughter and affection colouring the atmosphere. She promptly burst into tears because to her it was as if she was in *The Waltons*.

'I realised that was exactly what I was after. I just wanted to be cuddled and hugged and loved.' It was to have a lasting effect on her.

She says now, 'It's obvious I missed out on my childhood. What I want to do now is make as much money as quickly as possible so I can have a house in the country and ride quad bikes and horses all day. I want to spend a lot of time with my kids, sit round the table every night and make Sunday roast and grow nice flowers.'

CHAPTER SEVEN

LILY ON HOLIDAY

'I was working in that record shop, selling
Es and being bad.'

Lily was 15 and had finished school. It was summer and her future looked uncertain. But she didn't care, because she had a holiday planned and the destination would play a major part in Lily's future – both career-wise and as a person. Lily was going to Ibiza.

Despite its rich history, in the summer Ibiza is Europe's hedonistic clubbing capital. During the hottest months of the year the island is besieged by party-going tourists who take advantage of its scenic beauty, heat and wild nightlife. It is a hotbed of debauchery and drugs.

The fact that Lily wanted to go there was unsurprising. Music was playing a major part of her life. While she was still listening to her parents' music collection, she was starting to get into dance music in a big way – and Ibiza's heritage for dance would be the perfect education for her. And then of course there were the drugs.

Back in 1997, at the age of 12, Lily had attended the Glastonbury Festival. It wasn't her first encounter with the annual event as she had been going every year since she was 'about five months old' with Keith and Joe Strummer. 'We used to go to festivals with him [Joe] every year and he'd always play lots of hits, a lot of the older stuff, not really his music, but it gave me a musical education which I'm really grateful for.' But this time was different. For a start, she went without her dad, after running away from home and joining up with friends. It was here that she took marijuana and ecstasy for the first time. 'I had definitely started taking weed. I took my first E in 1997 at the Chemical Brothers set at Glastonbury; I didn't see it as anything special because it was all I knew.'

She couldn't wait to go to Ibiza as it would be full

of like-minded people who were up for a laugh, enjoying the music she likes. Lily could act the age she wanted to act. She had always resented family holidays but believed this would be different. 'Growing up was not glamorous at all,' she said. 'All my mates would be going on holiday abroad and we would always end up in this poxy caravan. I remember thinking, Can't we have a normal holiday like everyone else?'

In fact caravan holidays weren't exactly popular with the rest of the family either, after a bizarre incident in 1998. Lily and her brother Alfie were holidaying with their father in a horse-drawn Romany caravan. The horse reared up and crashed through the window of an oncoming van. Alfie was thrown clear; Lily – who was lying down – was unaffected. But Keith was not so lucky, as he later told a journalist: 'I managed to get a chain wrapped around my foot. It nearly tore my foot off, but snapped, and an iron bar hit me in the mouth and knocked four teeth out.'

So Ibiza it was. Lily felt at home, relaxed and assured in the hedonistic environment – and among people she understood and who understood her. She didn't need to be anyone but herself. And she was starting to come out of her shell in a big way.

'When I was 15 I kissed a 35-year-old stripper called Cheryl at Space in Ibiza. She had a necklace saying she'd won Stringfellows Stripper of the Year contest and she was kind of showing it off. It was a proper snog,' she admitted. Despite the same-sex experiment, Lily repudiated any suggestion that she is gay, insisting, 'The weirdest rumour I ever heard about myself was that I'm a lesbian.'

In her mind it was all playful fun. She spent the summer happy at first, popping 'millions of pills' and enjoying 'hanging out with strangers'. In Ibiza, far away from the stresses of London, she could be the grown-up she had always wanted to be. She would hang out in record shops, talk music all day with older men and spend a large part of her holiday on her own on a white beach, reading a book. It was bliss.

She was enjoying it so much she didn't want to go home. As the time to head back to London approached, Lily called her mother and begged her to let her stay, making wild promises that she would stay with friends. Alison reluctantly agreed. Overjoyed, Lily headed out again to the nearest club.

Unbeknown to Alison, far from being liberated, Lily was in fact getting more lost with each passing day. The friends Lily said she would be staying with would of course turn out to be non-existent, and instead she stayed in a hostel in San Antonio while working at a nearby record shop. 'I told her I was staying with friends for a week, but I ended up being there an extra month. I wasn't staying with friends, I was in a hostel by myself, working for this record shop called Plastic Fantastic and selling Es.'

And at night, after her stint in the shop, Lily was selling ecstasy at nightclubs. She enthused: 'I had nothing better to do. I was working in that record shop, selling Es and being bad.' She later admitted she wasn't the best drug dealer as 'I spent too much time trying out my own merchandise.'

To some, it may have looked like an astonishing cry for help; for Lily herself, it was the first time she had managed to overshadow her wild siblings in the rebellion stakes. It was a classic case of a middle child making herself heard. 'I guess it was because my brother and sister were both quite crazy and I felt like it was my turn.' Her sister was 'a fucking nightmare who took loads of drugs' and her little brother was 'extremely demanding'. This was her time.

Looking back, Lily is unapologetic about her time in Ibiza, defiantly claiming, 'What I do in my private life is nobody's business and I don't feel I have to justify that. I have experimented with drugs. I am not ashamed of it and I'm not going to deny it.'

But the good times were not to last. At the age of just 15 she was experiencing the world in all its severity. Night after night this wild child would rave the night away high on her own supply. In Lily's mind this was just one big extended holiday but like all good trips away it had to end sometime – and hers did in quite a dramatic way.

Once again she was stuck in yet another Ibiza club, riding high on a drink- and drugs-fuelled binge when she started to get hassled by a group of guys. Trying to ignore their repellent behaviour, she made to get out of their way, but they weren't taking no for an answer. 'They pushed me up against a wall and tried to get all frisky with me.'

Luckily for Lily she was about to be saved – in more ways than one. The man who stepped in and took her away wasn't there just to rescue her from a group of guys – he saved her from herself and was also about to pave the way for Lily the pop star. His name was George Lamb and he would go on to become her manager.

After rescuing Lily, George took her for a drink and they talked all night about music. Plucking up the courage, she showed him some little pieces of lyrics she had written. She explains, 'I always wanted to do music but never really had the confidence to do it until my first manager, George Lamb, who I met out in Ibiza, encouraged me.'

George, who was already a rising A&R man in the music industry and would later manage Audio Bullys, liked the look and energy of this young, defiant songstress, who even then was displaying the trademark savvy that belied her young years. After meeting the next day to discuss his becoming her manager, Lily made clear her terms. She says now, 'I don't sign anything with my managers. I still haven't signed a management contract. I could walk away whenever I fancied. But I wouldn't. I think that management is purely on a trust basis, that's how it works. If you work well for me, then you get 20 per cent of my money. I don't see why you'd want to sign a contract really, they're the only ones who'd win out of it.'

The terms were agreed but first George had to get Lily out of Ibiza. He knew this was no place for a young girl and took her back to her apartment to collect her things. When Lily wasn't looking, he stole her phone and called her mum to tell her that he had booked her daughter on a plane so she could sort herself out.

Lily didn't mind: she was coming home a singer.

CHAPTER EIGHT

THE SETBACK

'There's no money in it if you don't write your own songs.' GEORGE LAMB

With a manager to her name, Lily approached her father with the news that she wanted to be a singer. Keith was happy his once-aloof daughter had a goal, and although he knew it was a ruthless and fickle industry, he recognised his daughter's talents and musical influences as genuine.

Although Lily would soon get annoyed with the constant rumours and accusations that she is only famous because of her father, he did play a major part in securing her first deal.

Lily was glad of his savvy, enthusiasm and music contacts – especially in the London guitar band scene. Keith would go out of his way for his daughter in an attempt to launch her career. He would constantly book studio time for Lily and pull together his resources so she could perform with session musicians including members of the late Ian Dury's Blockheads.

Meanwhile, Lily was still with her boyfriend Lester and he was impressed with the lengths Keith was going to to make Lily's biggest dream come true. 'Keith's really cool and one of the funniest guys I know. He and Lily are really close. If it weren't for him she wouldn't be a success. They were always at studios together making music,' said Lester.

Armed with a collection of songs and a driven determination, Lily met bosses from London Records. After hearing a collection of her material, they agreed she had a blossoming songwriting talent. They were impressed and Lily secured her first record deal.

To celebrate Lily went out with Lester. The night was a wild one – champagne flowed as Lily celebrated with gusto, believing she had finally made it. The pair continued to drink, then mixed the booze with ecstasy and cannabis.

In the early hours of the morning they staggered to a taxi. 'Lily was wasted. She suddenly went green. She wound the window down as we were driving through Piccadilly Circus and threw up on the street. The taxi driver wanted to stop but she just pulled her head back in, grinned and told him to keep going,' recalled Lester.

London was a semi-independent label affiliated with record company Polygram until the label's head honcho, Roger Ames, moved to Warner Music Group and took London Records with him. Bizarrely, Keith Allen played a sound engineer called Roger Ames in the 2002 film *24 Hour Party People*. Whether this is a strange coincidence, or if it played some part in Lily's being signed, no one has ever revealed.

Meanwhile, bosses at London had high hopes that this talented, streetwise urchin would be a success, but they just didn't know what to do with her.

The songs Lily recorded for them were different from anything that would end up on her debut album, *Alright, Still*. There were no ska-tinged pop songs – instead there was much more of a folk influence to her music. It didn't go down well with the studio. And Lily herself wasn't very impressed because she was singing other people's songs. 'It was like modern UK folk music,' she revealed. She hopes the tracks never surface and is astonished they have not yet been released to a baying public desperate to hear anything she has lent her name to – but fears they soon will.

Another avenue the label was keen to explore was teaming Lily with other girls and forming an altogether different kind of girl band. They wanted a group based on music rather than looks, and one that would represent the real London with a strong urban, multicultural and streetwise vibe. Lily denies this band would become the Sugababes, but they did come out soon after, from the same music label and with the exact same ethos that was pitched to Lily.

At the time, Lily was totally opposed to the idea. There was no way she would share her talents in a group. She felt she deserved to be the centre of attention after living so long in the shadow of her disruptive siblings and famous father, and enduring her stifling education. It was her time to take centre stage – and it would only be on her terms and with music she actively played a part in making.

It's tempting to wonder what would have happened if Lily had indeed joined the Sugababes. There is no doubt the feisty band are a cut above the usual manufactured girl pop group. They are streetwise, savvy young women with singing talent and individuality, but would Lily have fitted in? It's doubtful she would have lasted long. How would the band famed for infighting and an almost revolving door of members have taken to this firecracker of a pop peer? It's an intriguing question.

Mutya, Keisha and Lily would have been, in theory at least, a mighty pop combo. But the sheer closeness of Mutya and Keisha – they even had their own secret language – would probably have forced Lily back into her shell. She could only be a force to be reckoned with if she felt there was no competition. And she would never be sold on the idea of joining a manufactured act and singing other people's songs.

Speaking at a launch party to promote her album in 2006, Lily said, 'I don't do this for the press. I do it for the music. If I did it for the press I would've got a record deal from my dad four years ago and I wouldn't have written any of my own songs. I would be prancing around taking my clothes off and singing cover versions, which I don't do. And going to loads of film premieres, which I don't do. It doesn't interest me. I don't care what people's views are.'

She also remembered one of the very first things her manager George said to her: 'There's no money in it if you don't write your own songs.'

This strict belief would pay dividends a few years later, but at the moment London Records was having trouble recognising what Lily could do for them. They eventually let her go, amid accusations that the label couldn't find a place for such a unique talent in a climate of easily manageable pop stars.

It was 2002 and there were no The Streets, Arctic Monkeys or other acts that put music before image. It was an era of pop clones and record companies were looking for acts that could give them quick fixes.

A former staff member at London Records told the *Daily Star* exactly what happened with Lily: 'We couldn't see her developing into the full package and her image wasn't right. Back then, she had a funny face and it all looked too challenging. We wanted pretty girls who were instantly marketable. So we got rid of her because she wasn't one of those.'

As the newspaper columnist Joe Mott saw it, 'Remember the fat, spotty girl at school who sent you a Valentine which you tore up in front of your mates? Imagine seeing her now looking like Cheryl Tweedy and being driven around in a Ferrari by a hunk who is liked by children and is nice to old ladies. That's how her old label bosses are feeling now.'

Lily was lucky to escape from that climate, but at the time it was a devastating loss. The London bosses had failed to recognise true talent because they were too busy looking at pie charts and data reports in their bid to mould yet another aspiring singer into an identikit pop puppet.

However, Lily refused to believe this was the end of her music career. She kept persevering with her lyric writing and soaked up more and more music. But she found it hard to stay motivated. She claims she left her record deal with a bit of cash and soon was just lazing around her house all day.

'The thing is, I had loads of money 'cos I'd had a record deal that came to a standstill and I took them to court so I had this bank account full of cash. I'd get up in the morning and didn't have anything to do so I thought, Fuck it, might as well smoke a joint. Then I'd sit on the bed and probably go to sleep for a couple more hours. Wake up. *Neighbours*. Listen to music in the afternoons: ragga, drum'n'bass, jungle. Sometimes I'd get the *Racing Post* in the morning and sit in my bed watching Channel Four Racing smoking weed all day.'

However, the money wouldn't last as long as she had hoped and soon the teenager who hated institutions and authority would have to find a normal job. 'My mum's not a handout woman. She always said, "If you want to go and buy expensive dresses and shoes, then go and earn a penny,"' recalled Lily.

She soon had spells working as a barmaid and at a PR company and even briefly as a florist – which, bizarrely, she enjoyed and became quite skilled at flower arranging. 'I did this course in it before the music thing worked out. I ended up working in this florist's for a few months.' She would often give her friends tips she had picked up from her new skill: 'Don't mix country flowers with exotic foliage. It's a common mistake that a lot of people make.'

However, she didn't last long in the job as she struggled with the early starts at four in the morning. At that hour, the hard-partying Lily was hoping to get to bed after a night clubbing, not to be starting her day, and she admitted, 'It was nice for a while, but I couldn't cope with getting up at 4am to buy stock and being told what to do.'

She still needed money for her upkeep, the occasional luxury buy and the many parking tickets she was accruing. And with a hiatus in her music career and her refusal to keep a normal job for long, she would end up stealing her mother's credit card. 'I was a bit of a kleptomaniac when I was 18. I went around Harvey Nichols with my mum's credit card. I got a £900 Marc Jacobs handbag. I also put all my parking tickets on my mum's card – £6,500 worth. I had to pay that all back.'

Eventually she lost her licence after drink-driving one night. And her ill-advised attempts to try to use her beauty on the law certainly didn't help her cause. 'I tried to charm this officer at the station, going, "Been here all night?" And he said, "I just arrested you…"' She would use the loss of her car as one of the many true-life incidents that light up her songs.

Lily was at breaking point. She was finally beginning to accept that her career was at a standstill. 'I had doors slammed in my face from lots of labels. It was because I was going out every weekend getting pissed and because I was my dad's daughter – that worked against me.'

Keith is convinced that that stage of her life was crucial, as it helped build her character. He says, 'I'm really proud because she spent two years' sleeping on friends' floors, doing all sorts of jobs and made it work by herself. It used to annoy her that they were calling her "Keith's daughter" because she did it on her own. But now we both think it's hilarious. I've got an autobiography coming out and I'm going to call it *By Lily Allen's Dad* 'cos she's more famous than me. She's brilliant. When she plays live it blows your mind. She couldn't get a deal at first, maybe because of my name, but she basically said, "Fuck you" to the record companies and did it anyway by putting her stuff on MySpace.'

Lily wasn't to know it but she was close to getting a second chance at a music career – but there would be one more setback.

CHAPTER NINE
BREAKDOWN

> 'I had met the boy who I thought was the love of my life, but he dumped me. I fell to pieces – trying to make him take me back, trying to make it work.'

By the beginning of 2003 Lily and Lester had been going out for nearly two years and it was becoming serious. They decided to start living together in a one-bedroom flat in London. It should have been a happy communion but cracks were starting to appear in their relationship. 'We started rowing about stupid things like not ringing each other when we were supposed to or whose turn it was to do the laundry,' remarked Lester.

They were relationship troubles common for new couples who move in together, but Lily was worried. Lester was starting to have doubts too and decided they needed to take a break from each other and have some breathing space. 'I organised a trip to Thailand with a mate. I was supposed to come back after a few months and we were supposed to fall into each other's arms and everything was supposed to be brilliant. But it just didn't work out like that,' he said.

While Lester was in Thailand they would argue over the phone and Lily would need constant reassurance that they were still a couple. One night the same question was being asked after another row, and Lester decided to call the relationship off. They were both in tears.

'I had a very miserable time in 2003,' admitted Lily. 'I had met the boy who I thought was the love of my life – but he dumped me. It's a situation many girls will relate to. I was really young and in love. I fell to pieces – trying to make him take me back, trying to make it work. It was a horrible time.'

It had been so different 18 months before when they met for the first time in London after occasionally bumping into each other when they were young children in County Kildare, Ireland.

They quickly realised they were into the same music and knew the same people, so it was only a matter of time before they were coming across each other regularly at trendy venues the End and the Notting Hill Arts Club, where they would watch up-and-coming DJs trying to make their mark in the music world.

'I fancied her straight away,' Lester says. 'Who wouldn't?' It took weeks, however, for the pair to get together. It finally happened when they were queuing to get into a party. The London weather was atrocious, and they stood there shivering as rain battered down on them. Needing a respite from the bitter cold, they snuggled up to each other, and realising there was a connection, they had their 'first snog'.

Both of them were drug users, constantly taking 'ecstasy and smoking loads of dope – our whole crowd was. For us it was no big deal,' enthused Lester. But Lily put her foot down when it came to heroin, as she feared dabbling in the Class A drug would turn her into an addict. 'I've never done that drug. I have the feeling that if I tried to do heroin just once, I'd decide this is what I'm meant to do with my life – be a heroin addict.'

And Lester insists that during their time together

he never saw her take cocaine – despite the furore she caused with an ill-placed comment after 'Smile' topped the charts. 'If she tried it, it wasn't when we were together.'

Drugs did play a major part in their relationship, though. Lester recalls one such moment in 2003 when they had both been taking ecstasy in a tent at the Glastonbury Festival. Lester admitted, 'We were pretty high. I remember having sex in the tent in the middle of the day and her younger brother Alfie coming in. He screamed and we fell about laughing.'

It wasn't the first time Alfie would interrupt the amorous pair in an intimate situation. When they started dating Lily was sharing a room with her younger brother, and when Lester stayed over they 'had to have sex in silence because her bunk bed was inches beneath her younger brother's bed'.

'We'd get high first by rolling a joint and blowing the smoke out of her bedroom window so her mum wouldn't smell it. We had to put our hands over each other's mouths,' revealed Lester. They were just a couple of teenagers getting into innocent scrapes and falling in love.

Lily had high hopes Lester was the one. He was the first person to bring stability to her life and Lily loved being with him. When they broke up Lily understandably took it hard. It was the last thing she needed after just losing her record deal ('My dream was gone') and making the decision earlier to come off drugs.

She had begun undergoing therapy earlier in the year after realising she had carried the burden of pent-up aggression during her youth for too long. She underwent cognitive behavioural therapy to rectify her anger and depression. It was a brave step to take, so the break-up couldn't have come at a worse time. 'At the age of 17 and 18 all these emotions are coming through and it's hard to cope. I started to get depressed and anyone who suffers from depression knows that it can soon get so bad that you can't get out of bed.'

It was to get much worse. Lily was devastated after being dumped by Lester and she had nothing to fall back on. Her music career looked dead and buried, even if she was still working on her songwriting. She could handle the failure of her pop ambitions when she had Lester. Now she had nothing. 'I'd fallen in love, that was holding me together and once he left me I was like, "Well, this is just the end now."'

She was at her mum's house when she decided to end her life. 'I took about 35 sleeping pills at my mum's … and woke up in hospital. I'd just thought, I don't wanna be here tomorrow, when nothing else is ever gonna happen. I was coming down off all the drugs I'd been taking for years and felt really alone. I remember thinking, I just don't have the energy any more to try.'

It was a shocking incident and a close shave, and it immediately spurred her parents into action. Not that they needed to convince Lily. She knew what had to be done. 'It triggered me to sort my life out,' she recalled. 'It was then that I checked into the Priory. That was really tough as I was an emotional mess.' Lily found the experience devastating. She had been before many times, but only as a guest visiting her mum or dad during their stints in rehab. This time it would be more than a fleeting visit.

When she left, Lily was still struggling to regain confidence, admitting that 'when I came out of there it took me a while to get my life on track. I even tried to get back with the same boyfriend, which just shows how stupid we can all be.'

Lester didn't know much about her spell in rehab and only heard bits and pieces about what had happened, insisting, 'Eighteen months is a long time when you're only young. I heard from friends back home that she had a sort of breakdown and I felt

Lily flashes her trademark smile after performing on NBC's *The Today Show* in New York, April 2007.

Top left: Lily's mum, Alison Owen, cast her in the film *Elizabeth* as a lady in waiting when she was just thirteen years old. She has been determined to succeed ever since.

Top right: Lily and dad Keith didn't see much of each other during her early childhood. They have a good relationship now and are pictured arriving together at the 2007 Brit Awards...

Below left: ... before going on to an afterparty!

Below right: Lily manages to combine her mum's strong work ethic with her dad's fondness for partying!

© WENN

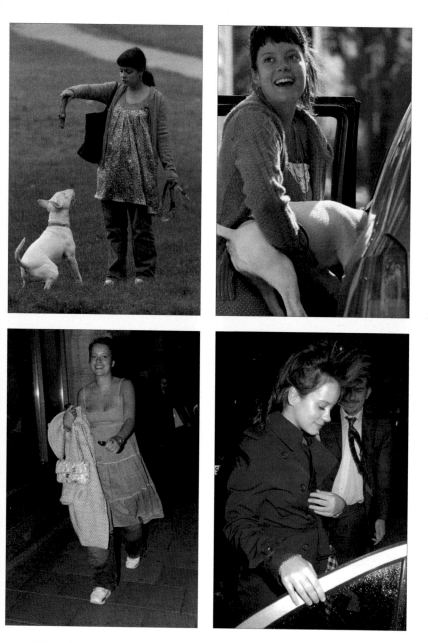

Top: Lily adores her dog, Maggie May, and loves to take her for a walk on Primrose Hill when she's at home in London.

Below: When you're as big a star as Lily, even taking a walk down the street or getting into a car is newsworthy for the tabloids! © *WENN*

Lily admits that fame can have its downsides, and cites being photographed when she's doing daily chores *(top left)* as one of the more testing sides to celebrity. Taking a nap on a picnic bench at the Bestival weekend music festival on the Isle of Wight *(top right)* before taking the main stage by storm *(opposite)*.

Below: Negotiating the press with boyfriend Seb Chew as they enter London's Wardour Club. That night, there was some commotion between Lily and the photographers outside. © *WENN*

Music is Lily's first love. She's a talented singer-songwriter and also turns her hand to DJing *(top)*.

Below left: Performing in LA's Wiltern Theatre during her May 2007 tour.

Below right: Lily sold out the Hammersmith Apollo, the last stop on a UK tour before she took America by storm. Lily's raw and rousing performance included covers of Blondie and Kaiser Chiefs hits. © *WENN*

Social networking website MySpace was key to Lily's early success, with fans discovering her profile and joining her as friends in their hundreds of thousands. Fans from around the world were able to listen online to her music, making Lily's following truly international. Here she is pictured performing in Amsterdam (*top*), Baden-Baden (*bottom left*) and Seattle (*bottom right*).

Lily after performing 'LDN' at a record store in London.

awful about it. I heard she went into the Priory but I wasn't around so I don't know just how bad it was.'

Looking back at their relationship he says, 'She's a sweet girl and I loved her. I still think she's cool and we still talk. We just fell out of love. We're both still young and it was the first time either of us had been properly in love. Yeah, I suppose we are the loves of each other's lives and it was brilliant while it lasted.'

Lester would still have a big part to play in Lily's life. Her spell in rehab would give her the impetus to try again at a musical career, and her break-up with Lester would inspire the song 'Smile', which tells the story of a woman enjoying seeing an ex-boyfriend suffer. It is that sort of inner belief that makes Keith sure his daughter will never be a serial rehab patient like her mother or father. 'She's got too much of an old head on young shoulders. She will be fine.'

And she certainly would be. The next stage of her life was eagerly awaiting her and it would give Lily everything she wanted – but only if she stuck to her principles.

CHAPTER TEN

DOING IT FOR HERSELF

> 'I want to make music that doesn't compromise any of my morals.'

Lily was born of famous parents, and that brings with it a host of insecurities to deal with, so it's not surprising there would be occasions where she would meet and relate to like-minded people from similar backgrounds. One such person was Peaches Geldof.

Born in 1989, Peaches is the daughter of political activist and singer Sir Bob Geldof and TV presenter Paula Yates. Like Lily, she is the middle child in a family overshadowed by famous parents. As she did with her childhood friend Miquita Oliver, Lily had found someone else who knew where she was coming from. In fact, Peaches had it far worse than Lily. Both her parents were far more famous – and notorious – than Keith and Alison. Sir Bob was one of the figureheads of Live Aid, while her mother Paula was a troubled media personality who left Geldof for late rocker Michael Hutchence in 1995. Hutchence committed suicide in 1997, and Paula died three years later from an accidental heroin overdose. As a result Peaches grew up in the harsh spotlight of the media.

Here was someone Lily could relate to, but rather than build a secure clique for themselves, their friendship – if you could call it that – would be one of envy and bitterness. Lily would hang around Peaches for a while but it was tough for her because all she could see was a very young girl and her equally young friends doing well for themselves. They were as rebellious as Lily but they also had a sense of composure that wasn't a mask for insecurity. They were genuinely confident girls and Lily realised that time 'was running out for her'. It made her realise she had to do something with her life before it was too late.

Because of Lily's experiences with her father, she found it hard to relate to girls. If she was at a typical

London nightclub with girls dancing around their handbags, Lily would be at nearby table laughing at them with a group of guys. She was far more comfortable with boys than she ever was with girls. 'All my friends would be a group of boys and it would be very much like the situation with my dad – all of us shouting and chanting at football matches.

'If a skinny blonde girl comes walking into a pub I'm immediately hating her. I don't want to talk to her because I would feel threatened by her. And that's not a good thing.'

That all changed when she sat down to start writing music for her second attempt at a break-through. After the disappointment and heartbreak of the failure of her contract with London Records, Lily was finally ready to try again and she was determined to make it work this time. She had started to think more and more about her potential audience and what they would be, and she was concerned about her role as a strong female.

She said, 'It's funny, because one of the main markets for buying music is 15- to 24-year-old girls, and so it's really strange that there aren't any females directly trying to appeal to that age group, or trying to talk to that age group on a lyrical level. I think that they try to make bands with the right amount of hair gel, make sure that the lead singer is quite good-looking and that the bass player has an air of mystery, and Bob's your uncle. It's odd that there aren't any females doing that, especially not young females.'

Lily devoured her record collection. She studied intensely what worked and what she could genuinely achieve.

'As a teenager I got into hip-hop, jungle and ska. I was desperate to be a dancehall queen. I was so jealous of M.I.A. [Maya Arulpragasam, the British singer of Sri Lankan origin who captured the Jamaican dancehall sound perfectly] when she came out. So it was about finding what was acceptable, but still staying true to what I believed in. With ska, and bands like the Specials, there were always white people attached to it,' she admitted.

She took what she had learned when she was 13 and studied jazz, listening to legends Blossom Dearie and Ella Fitzgerald – 'I guess that's where a lot of my melody writing would come from' – coupling it with genres ranging from urban and ska to bands, including 'The Specials, Rip, Rig and Panic, T. Rex – possibly the best band ever, ever! – the Slits, Blondie and Wreckless Eric. Oh, and Kate Bush when she was my age, Prince and Eminem.' She added a touch of Manchester music from the days of legendary club Hacienda, like the Stone Roses, 808 State and the Smiths, to create a strong range of influences that she would end up poring over in great detail.

Lily felt that Manchester was the perfect location for her comeback. She knew she had to get out of London because there were so many distractions. 'Going out and getting drunk all the time isn't great for the creative juices. So I persuaded the record company to let me try some new places.'

Her manager George Lamb agreed and she was promptly dispatched to do some demos with production team Future Cut, consisting of Darren Lewis and Tunde Babalola. Lewis and Babalola first met while promoting rival club nights in Manchester before making a name for themselves in drum'n'bass in the late 1990s. Future Cut would do the beats, while Lily would work on the melodies and lyrics.

The young singer was understandably intimidated when she met the pair. They were big personalities and when they interrogated her about her past, she 'just lied and told them I'd been writing since I was little. I blagged it.' When they asked to see what she was made of, she ad-libbed about an ex-boyfriend, singing whatever words and melodies came into her head.

Lily looks back at the encounter with embarrassment, saying, 'They told me we needed a middle eight, I went, "Right", then I had to call my manager and ask what a middle eight was.' The song she was working on would eventually be 'Smile' – the song that would make her famous.

Although the technical jargon may have confused her she was displaying a natural sense of rhythm and musical intelligence. 'The first song I wrote was 'Smile'. What came into my head was "Smile, smile", and I thought, Well, I like that but it's too happy, it's too nice. Darren said, "Twist the lyrics a bit." So I thought, How can I make "smile" sound horrible? And then I thought, When I see you cry it makes me smile! That set the tone for everything.'

That simple arrangement changed everything. It unlocked something in Lily. She was a natural, sharp-witted lyricist. The years of observation had played their part, and she now realised the influences of her past were coming to fruition.

'I've always been an observational person. Friends get irritated with me in social situations, because I can't concentrate until I know exactly what's going on in every corner of the room, then I feel comfortable.'

While working on her new material in Manchester

she stayed with her father's friend, notorious Happy Mondays member and *Celebrity Big Brother* contestant Mark 'Bez' Berry. It was to be a memorable stay.

One day Bez, realising he had to go to London for a night, asked Lily to look after his two sons, Jack and Arlo, for the day. As she remembers it, 'He said, just put them in a cab to school, make sure they've got their packed lunches, so I was like, "Yeah, cool" and then he didn't come back for a week! He'd ended up in Dublin or somewhere ... Still, it makes a good anecdote,' she laughed.

Impromptu babysitting episodes aside, she loved working with her new collaborators because she felt they were on the same page. They weren't trying to make her something she was not, and in return, unlike other pop stars who would publicly claim that everything originated from them, Lily was happy to give credit where credit was due and admit this was a total collaboration.

'I spent two and a half years working really, really hard trying to make a respectable pop record that people who I respect would listen to and not be offended by. It was a time when people like Rachel Stevens and Madonna were recreating 1980s electro pop, and although that was a cool thing at the time, I wanted to do something that was much more organic. I took a whole load of my records and went through them with Darren and Tunde, finding stuff that I liked and mentioning samples. I rely heavily on my producers. We all go into the studio and listen to a bunch of seven-inches: either they'll write something from scratch or we'll just sample a record straight away. While they are doing that I'll come up with an idea for the song, a word will come out, and I'll either write a verse or a chorus, whatever will come first.'

Showing remarkable natural songwriting ability, Lily would be inspired by the beats her producers created and would come up with lyrics in 'an hour and a half, tops. Then I'd improvise the melody later. If it's good, it's usually easy'.

Lily is also modest enough to know her limitations. She is happy to admit she was not a 'music geek' and didn't know a bass from a guitar but was 'a music enthusiast. If I hear something I like, I go and get it and I listen to it until I'm sick of it.

'A lot of female artists, and male ones for that matter, are boring singers who don't say anything. Certainly not to my generation. With the kind of music I do you have to be direct and quite literal. I don't play an instrument, which really makes me focus on the vocal melody, and the lyrics are incredibly important to me. I don't want to be part of a scene, the whole idea of that makes me feel sick, and most of the music I listen to is by outsider figures, which is where I feel happiest.'

With the help of her collaborators Lily quickly realised that songwriting came naturally to her. And typically for her, she would feel guilty about it. 'I have worked hard but at the same time some of it is down to having the gift of the gab. There are a lot of musicians who have played for 15 years and have never got recognition. I have worked hard, but at the same time it has come naturally to me. I just feel guilty that things have happened so smoothly.' And it was smooth, considering her last recording deal, but she still felt that the more collaborators she had, the better.

Super-hot producer Mark Ronson (who has worked with Christina Aguilera) would be next on Lily's wish list – and as usual she got what she wanted.

She had finally got over Lester and started a relationship with DJ Seb Chew. Seb co-promoted YoYo at the Notting Hill Arts Club every Thursday and knew a lot of influential people making their voices heard in the music industry. The club night was a media darlings' event and everyone wanted to be there.

Luckily for Lily, she heard that Ronson would be at the club. Seizing her chance, she attempted to get some demos of her work to him. She shyly approached him and handed over a tape. It was at that precise moment that she realised for the first time that it wasn't about the music – she just wanted to be signed. And he was the person who could do that.

Ronson politely took the recording but it was to be a couple of months before he listened to it. And when he eventually did, he was transfixed. He remembers, 'It was like, "Oh, my mate's girlfriend gave me a tape of her music – throw it in the pile." I never took it seriously. Then I popped it in and I was like, "I love this." I would have bought it that day if I'd heard it on the radio, so I paid for her to come over immediately.'

'The next thing I knew I was on a plane to New York,' recalled Lily. It was to have an enormous impact on her career. Ronson loved working with her, and with his influence she got her second record deal, at Regal Records – an imprint of EMI – in September 2005. Lily was delighted, but remained sceptical after what had happened the last time.

However, she enjoyed working with the songwriter they had given her – Greg Kursten.

Kursten, who worked on several stand-out tracks on what would be *Alright, Still*, says she is an easy collaborator and recalls, 'She was also open to hearing stuff that I brought in. On some songs I brought in tracks. And we ended up cutting them up when we were in the room together. We didn't overthink anything, just finished it in a day and we moved on.'

Lily was in a confident mood. When the record company enquired how many potential singles the album could generate, she looked at them confused. 'I find it funny, that record-company-speak of "How many singles have you got?" I mean, why don't you just try and do an album of twelve singles, instead of three? So that's what I did.'

While she was making her album, she was given an enormous opportunity by her record label. Robbie Williams's new album was coming out and they needed backing vocals on a couple of songs, 'Lovelight' and 'King of the Bongo'.

Because Mark Ronson was producing the album he suggested Lily, and she came quickly on board. Here she was, young, scruffy Lily, about to be elevated into the big time; typically, it didn't impress her.

Robbie Williams represented what Lily hated about celebrities. While recording her part on the album she was stunned to see the pop star have one of his lackeys put artificial sweetener in his coffee and stir it while he just sat there. 'Talk about being affected by fame,' she recalled.

But the experience would be a good one for her, and for Robbie. Despite the album's lukewarm reception, its credibility was boosted on its release in summer 2006 because of Lily's input. She said at the time, with tongue firmly in cheek, 'I sang on a few tracks, which has worked out pretty well for Robbie, I'd say. I mean, me being a No. 1 artist and all.'

At that moment Lily couldn't have hoped for anything more. She was collaborating with talented people, her music was coming along well and she was being asked to work with some of the biggest names in music. It had all happened within months of her being signed.

But in November 2005 everything stalled. The record company told Lily they didn't think 'the direction of the demos was quite right'. They were delaying the release of her debut album until January 2007.

She recalled, 'It wasn't that they weren't supportive. They just didn't think it was ready –

because it wasn't. They were trying things out, like putting me with more mainstream producers and top-line writers because they didn't think my melodies were quite there – it wasn't sonically "pop-sounding" enough or whatever.'

Lily was crushed. They wanted to take her hard-earned music and dilute it for more mainstream audiences. They wanted her to work with talented songwriters like Cathy Dennis, who wrote 'Toxic' for Britney Spears. It was never going to be the right fit.

Surprisingly, Lily agreed to do whatever the record company wanted. 'I tried it! I'm not going to say I was always adamant. I didn't know that my stuff was good enough. I'm not like an uber-confident person who thinks she's amazing. If the people from the record company were telling me it's not good enough and I should be working with these people, I was like, "OK, cool, whatever," but it always sounded very contrived. I can't sit there and sing, "Ooh baby, you make me crazy, can I be your lady, baby?" It doesn't work.'

The situation looked bleak. It was going so well, but Lily knew from bitter experience what happens with record companies who aren't happy with what they have got. She feared everything was going to be taken away from her again, as it had been with

London Records – except that she had got so far this time and so close to creating her own sound. Just as she was about to give up hope for a second time, Lily stumbled across a social networking website that was to change everything for her. It was called MySpace.

CHAPTER ELEVEN

LILY LOGS ON

'I say what I say and the kids seem to love it.'

Set up in July 2003, MySpace has become an internet and social phenomenon. The networking site allows members to meet people, trade videos and pictures and, more importantly, upload music for everyone to hear – giving individuals and groups a platform to create their own online diaries in the form of blogs.

Music and MySpace began to mesh quite publicly at the time that Lily logged on in November 2005. Guitar band Arctic Monkeys became overnight sensations after thousands of fans logged on to their MySpace page to listen to and download their music.

Although the band now claims the online hysteria they prompted was purely accidental and not down to a master plan, it was a canny move and one that other record companies would soon replicate.

Using MySpace properly, record companies could generate astonishing word-of-mouth publicity and create a massive fan base months before singles were released. The possibilities were endless. However, it would take a 20-year-old girl from Hammersmith to fully open the industry's eyes to the new medium.

While other bands had become famous through MySpace, Lily was the first artist to utilise its services fully. By uploading her songs herself, sending out mix tapes to her fans and regularly blogging her fans with rants, anecdotes and information that is usually available to only the closest of friends, she quickly became crowned the Queen of MySpace.

But a lot of it was down to luck. Lily wasn't – at first anyway – using the internet as a revolutionary tool to stun the industry. 'I was just using it to find routes out to the countryside to the grandparents' house and to pay my congestion charge. I don't even know how long the internet's been around, but for me it only started becoming a part of everyday life in the past four or five years.

'It was totally unintentional the way that things happened with MySpace. I actually first set it up as a personal MySpace. After a few days of navigating the site, I realised you could have music, so I cancelled my personal account and started a new account, and it just kind of happened.'

Lily immediately recognised the potential of the internet as a vital tool for getting her music across to a bigger audience. 'The record industry has been run in a very straightforward way over the past ten years and I think record-company bosses are just coming to terms with how to open an email. You walk into record labels these days and there are more and more young people around because the older people don't understand the internet and how it works. That's where the music market is – on the internet.'

Another aspect that intrigued her was the concept of sharing her thoughts with her new-found fans. The blogging culture was tailor-made for Lily. For too long she had let her thoughts, feelings and aggression build up inside her. This was an ideal chance to stand on a cyber soapbox and spout forth anything that came into her head. She explained, 'I've been blogging for a long time. I'm quite an opinionated person, but I'd never written a diary before. I quite like it! Probably a lot of tastemakers and music journalists are getting pissed off with me writing on MySpace because it's essentially eliminating them from being tastemakers. It enables people to go out and make their own decisions. So I think it's really fun!'

Lily would later discover a drawback to documenting her feelings so openly and publicly. 'It definitely became annoying when I would write something and it would end up in the tabloids the next day, completely twisted around. It's like, fuck off.'

Airing her opinions was one thing but the real reason for using the site was to test the water with her music. She was confident of her tunes to an extent, but lacked the self-belief to stand up to her record company. She needed vindication from the people who mattered most: her potential fans.

'Over the past two years I had been doing demos and I probably had, like, seven or eight that I was confident enough to put on the page for people to hear. I started putting them up in November two months after I signed. I just kind of swapped them around. When we did "Nan, You're a Window Shopper", literally five minutes after we finished, it was on MySpace.'

Instantly, Lily became a cult sensation. Young girls became fascinated by the eclectic collection of sounds. It was a melting pot of influences and a musical representation of multicultural Britain. And they loved the pop pixie singing it. Her witty comments allowed people to see the inner workings of a pop star in the making in their most intimate form.

Three weeks after she set up her own MySpace account her manager phoned up. 'He said, "I think you ought to set this thing up, it's called MySpace or something", and I was like, "Already done it."'

But Lily is not being smug about it and is quick to defend her label: 'It wasn't like the record company didn't like my music, or they would never have signed me in the first place. But I don't think they thought [the music] was there yet, and MySpace just gave them more confidence. People at record companies are under so much pressure to perform these days that they try to over-think things a little. MySpace was a bit of relief for all of us because I was happy with what I was doing and I couldn't understand why everyone else didn't think it was there.'

Lily would spend two to three hours a day on the site chatting to her new friends. While it was obvious she was relishing being the centre of an enormous amount of attention, it was more than just a popularity contest.

'Fans need to have some emotional connection with an artist,' she later explained.

'All you have to do is look at the recent All Saints album [which flopped] to see that if they aren't connecting with you as a friend then it just doesn't work.

'People assume I have a team of monkeys doing the MySpace thing for me, but I don't. I do it all myself. There is nothing nicer than coming off the road, and being so, so tired and logging on to the internet and their thousands of people telling you how brilliant you are. It's brilliant.'

Three months after putting her songs on the site she realised things were getting far bigger than she anticipated. 'There were so many subscribers to the blog and so many people listening to the music – the plays were just going up and up and up,' she said.

The first inkling Polygram had that something special was happening was when the label's head of press, Murray Chalmers, began receiving calls from journalists demanding an interview with the online sensation. He had no idea who Lily Allen was.

Lily enthused, 'You know within a record company they have A&R and marketing and press and whatever. Obviously, A&R knew about me but nobody else in the record company did at that point.

And Murray was getting calls from people who were like, "We want to write about Lily," and he was like, "I don't know what you're talking about.'"

Journalists from the prestigious *Observer Music Monthly* magazine had to make five or six phone calls asking to interview Lily for an article about the influence of MySpace before Murray demanded to know what was going on.

'Murray was like, "OK, this is stupid. Now five people have called about this Lily girl, who the hell is she?" So he walked down to A&R and was like, "Have we got someone called Lily Allen on our books?" And they were like, "Oh yeah, she's this girl we got a few months ago." And that's kind of when it all started, and then three weeks later we got the offer for the cover on the *Observer* magazine.'

All this hype, and yet Lily and her music only existed on the worldwide web. She hadn't released any music and Regal had no plans to do so yet. To quench the media's thirst, Lily put out a limited seven-inch vinyl release of 'LDN' on 24 April 2006. The reason was simple and it showed her astute mind for business. 'We knew that we had to put out the limited release of "LDN". You can't really have all that press and not have the little tagline on the end that says, "'LDN' by Lily Allen, out on this date". So we did the limited edition just to have something that people could talk about and hold.' Because the MySpace thing was working so well, she convinced her record label to pay for 200 of them.

To keep her fans happy, Lily also made a series of mix tapes of her raw demos spliced with music she liked. 'It was something for me to do because my writing wasn't happening. Every night I'd spray all the covers, and they were individually numbered. And it was free. I hand-wrote everyone's addresses on the front and put them in the post and that kind of got people talking. And it was really good, because that was the time when they were trying to put me in with producers, and I'm not very good at articulating what I want with music, so it was really helpful to have the mix tape and say, "OK, this is the kind of music I like, these are my influences, so let's try to build off some of these things."'

By May 2006 her songs had been downloaded 1.3 million times and she had 24,000 friends on the site. The heads of her record label sat down with Lily and formulated a plan to seize the moment. They were looking at her growing fan base with astonishment and excitement. They rush-released her first single in July and told her the album couldn't wait till next year.

There was a problem, though. Lily was becoming addicted to the adulation being poured over her on her MySpace site. It was the truest vindication she ever had in life but it was hurting the album. It still needed a few more songs but Lily was more interested in going home and 'reading about how much people love me on MySpace.

'I'd read all the messages, "Oh you love me, great, great!" I was getting very excited about that, and I suddenly got writer's block. It was a really bad time for it to happen – everyone was getting excited on the back of the MySpace site and the album wasn't finished. So I decided to go to America and work with Greg Kursten to finish the album.'

Lily couldn't believe it. Just a few months earlier she had feared her career was over for the second the time, but now she was going to release her first single and was about to have her first cover shoot and there was an almighty buzz being generated about her. And the most satisfying aspect of it all was that she had done it for herself. No record company jargon, no marketing meeting and courting the press – just Lily armed with a collection of songs and music fans eager to hear something that was relevant to them.

CHAPTER TWELVE

LILY SMILES AT NO 1

'With the kind of music I do, you have to be direct.
I don't play as instrument, which really
makes me focus on the melody.'

There was a feverish anticipation surrounding Lily Allen in the media. The press had quickly latched on to the saucer-eyed songstress because she was a breath of fresh air compared with the pop clones spouting the media-trained soundbites that journalists were used to. She was feisty, opinionated and had talent to back up her mouthy outbursts. There was a genuine feeling that Lily could make the transition from media darling to a mainstream audience, with tabloid newspapers such as the *Sun* and *Daily Star* and trendy music magazines fighting over who saw her first.

Her first press coverage was on the cover of the

Observer Music Monthly in May. Lily jumped out of bed on the day the magazine came out and walked to the newsagents. She had 'been shitting myself about it for the whole week before it came out', but was delighted when she held the cover in her hand.

Looking at herself laughing exuberantly in a red ball gown on top of Primrose Hill, Lily was thrilled. After years of toiling with her musical aspirations and personal setbacks she was finally looking at the reward. Even her friends were amazed at how she had come off in the interview, joking, 'If I didn't know you were such a twat, I'd think you were quite cool.' She may not have been cool when she made her pals take a picture of her to the magazines, but she certainly was all smiles.

And on paper she had every right to be happy. Her forthcoming debut single, 'Smile', was being tipped as a potential smash and she had just played her first gig at the Notting Hill Arts Club, where a thousand people turned up at the 200-capacity venue. 'It was a bit fucked up because the record label people were all like, "We're the most important, we need to get in," and Seb and Leo [the promoters] were going, "Fuck them, it's about the punters." It's heartbreaking when you're in a queue and you see a bunch of cunts in suits walk straight through the door. Although saying that, I never queue,' laughed Lily.

'The reason I hadn't performed live before was because I was really, really scared of doing it and I didn't know that I *could* do it. When I finally did it, the feeling was so great, and I found that I could do it quite well, and I just wanted to do it again. Now I love it; it's the favourite bit for me now.'

When it came to promoting the release of 'Smile', EMI needed to capitalise on the hype of MySpace. It had a sophisticated battle plan centred on a new website it had created for her.

The impressive new site was designed to capture Lily's personality and vibrancy and offered fans access to exclusive mix tapes, breaking news, blogs, free MP3 downloads and video footage. It was important that the new site complemented MySpace without replacing it and without alienating the friends Lily had worked so hard to gather. The label's digital media manager, Dan Duncombe, explained, 'With this campaign we ensured that Lily remains true to her online roots and her success through MySpace. With nearly 40,000 friends, MySpace is one of the most important, direct and targeted promotion platforms we have.'

A WAP offshoot enabled fans to buy ringtones of

Lily's songs and enter competitions to win gig tickets and her trademark Nike trainers and Chopper bikes. Murray Chalmers masterminded the press publicity campaign. His job had been made easy, as he explained, 'It started quite naturally, because a few press people picked up on her from MySpace. It was really unusual, because I didn't call people, I just sat back and let it happen.'

Because much of the press, particularly the broadsheets, had already picked up on Lily and run interviews as early as March 2006, Chalmers could focus his attentions on specialist magazines in the fashion and music press to widen her appeal. 'It was a national campaign, we didn't do much regional stuff as we started off really high. We decided what we wanted and we got pretty much all of it. I don't think there was a problem. She is doing regional now because she's touring. But with Lily, because it happened so quickly, we did national straight away.'

The first midweek position for 'Smile' was looking good. It was heading to No. 1. Lily was stunned, but was quick to retain her composure and adopt her usual modest stance, 'It's fucking amazing for me now to be in the position I am, and be No. 1 in the midweeks, knowing full well that all the A&R men

I've been going into meetings with for the last three years will now be kicking themselves.'

When she performed on *Top of the Pops* she met a familiar face. The Kooks frontman Luke Pritchard and Lily were at school together in their early teens. 'We used to rehearse Green Day songs when we were 14, so it was quite a cool moment being sat in the BBC courtyard together waiting to go on *Top of the Fucking Pops*.'

When Lily was finally declared No. 1 with 'Smile' her main memory was her MySpace account. Because she had kept in such close contact with her fan base, the enormity of her success became very clear instantly. 'My MySpace just went insane. It was first thing in the morning where I was but there were hundreds of comments and I thought, This is it now.'

But being in such a fast-paced industry, Lily didn't have long to celebrate her remarkable achievement. She had to rush off for an appearance at the annual Scottish festival T In The Park. Not that the pint-sized singer was going to let anyone forget who was top of the charts. The sun may have been shining in Scotland, but so was her career, and Lily was quick to point it out to anyone who came close to her, even members of rival bands. 'I was just walking around going, "I'm No. 1 and none of you are." They all fucking hated me, like, "Who is this obnoxious girl in a ball gown?"'

But if a few guitar bands' egos were bruised, no one could argue with Lily's success – certainly not the ten thousand people singing back to her when she played the chart topper later that night. 'It was an amazing experience,' she recalled.

That night would play another important part in Lily's life: it would reinforce her role as a strong woman in a male-dominated industry. She, Regina Spektor and Sandi Thom were the only female artists at the event, yet she had the top in the UK charts. Lily's underdog mentality and her belief that it's harder for empowered female singers to make their mark than men would rear its head countless more times before the year was out. She admitted: 'Being in this industry has turned me into a real feminist because it just angers me so much, the lack of respect.'

Lily was quickly making her mark. Even her B-sides were causing a stir. The song 'Cheryl Tweedy', in which Lily slyly dissects modern culture's obsessive quest for unattainable beauty, caused the real-life Cheryl to completely miss the satirical angle of the song. She gushed, 'I'm really flattered that Lily's written a track about me. I don't know why she sings about wanting to be as pretty as me, as she looks stunning. I'd like to look like her.'

Lily wasn't slow to point out her mistake, 'I don't want to look like Cheryl Tweedy! It's tongue-in-cheek. It's meant to be ironic. I don't have anything against her as a human being. It was a joke that not many people got. Of course, nobody really wants to look like Cheryl, they just think they do.'

Everything was rosy. Lily was having the time of her life – and the only black spot was when the subject of nepotism arose. It was a constant thorn in her side and was the one question guaranteed to wipe the smile from her face.

On one occasion, she answered back defiantly, 'Well, I've worked really hard for five years, my dad's never met anyone from my label, he's never even met my manager. It's annoying when people assume that you're handed something on a plate, when it's actually completely the opposite. They're all pussies in the record industry, they thought I was a risk. It's not a secret that I like to go out and have fun and also the music's quite reggaeish, and I'm a white middle-class girl, which they couldn't get their heads around. Anyway, if there's one famous person that's going to go against you, it's my dad. Unless I was Pete Doherty's daughter or something.'

Accusations of nepotism still crop up, and amazingly one brave journalist compared her life to that of Paris Hilton. 'That's so insulting to me. How can that be right?' said Lily. 'The thing is, she had already well established herself as being a celebrity, but I didn't use any of my connections to achieve what I achieved. Nothing. The people that got me into the studio are people that I met on holiday in Ibiza when I was 16 years old. Nothing to do with my family. Also, she comes from a multi-millionaire background. My dad's been in a couple of TV programmes and a couple of films, and my mum's a low-budget film producer. They're hardly the same backgrounds.'

But Lily knew what to expect. She was a shrewd operator and knew how the media worked. She didn't care about the accusations. She was the No. 1 artist in the country and the majority of people seemed enthralled by this doe-eyed urchin. Even the police were bringing Lily good news. She had got her driving licence back and treated herself to a trendy Mini Cooper S. 'It's just to keep me going until I can afford a Bentley Coupe!'

Lily was joking of course. The only money she had seen at this point was an advance when she signed, and most of that she handed over to her mother.

'Obviously, my mum subsidised me quite a lot then. My parents are quite middle class, but my dad's never given me any money. He's a fucker. The first thing I had to do when I signed my deal was pay my mum thousands of pounds. She'd kept tabs on everything she'd given me!' But while Lily hoped she would see more money, it was not the reason she got into the music business.

Privately, though, as a perennial worrier, she feared she would be dismissed as a one-hit wonder. The fears didn't go away after the success of 'Smile', but she needn't have worried. Her big mouth would ensure she had everyone's attention.

CHAPTER THIRTEEN

LILY'S BIG MOUTH

'I don't really say anything intentionally to hurt anybody's feelings. But at the same time, I have opinions on people and I don't really know how to hold back.'

It was supposed to be an innocuous interview. A harmless one-to-one between music's new sensation and the influential magazine *NME*. Lily was overjoyed at being asked to appear in its pages, as it was proof she had made it. The interview had started off well. Lily was being her usual self-deprecating and gobby self and was happy to speak openly about drugs and her past, when the conversation turned to drugs in the music industry.

It was to be a long, spirited talk on the topic. Lily remembered it well: 'And the next question after that was, "How are you going to celebrate your No. 1 this weekend?" And I went, "Oh, gak!" as a joke, because we just had this whole talk about drugs.'

It was a flippant comment delivered in Lily's typically dry tone. After the interview had ended, she thanked the interviewer and left, with no inkling about the controversy she had created. She wouldn't have to wait till the magazine came out before discovering her dry, acerbic humour wasn't suited to the cold and unforgiving world of print.

'They didn't print the previous part of the conversation, just the last line where I said I celebrated by taking coke. And then the PR person for their magazine called the tabloids and sold them the story.'

Lily was crushed. It was a cruel blow for her as she was still riding high on the adulation given her by the public and critics. The article had implied that she was serious about her joke. Media commentators were quick to point fingers and tut at Lily for being irresponsible and a bad role model for her young fans.

Seeking to control the situation before it got out of hand, Lily quickly apologised, 'I made a silly joke while being interviewed. I'm so sorry if I have disappointed any of you. I did not want to encourage youngsters to take drugs.'

Privately, though, she was seething. 'It really upset me, because I thought if there was one magazine that could take me seriously as a female artist and be responsible about it, it was the *NME*,' she fumed.

What annoyed her the most was the magazine's perceived hypocrisy. 'I mean, I read articles every week about boys in bands talking about actually consuming drugs themselves and nothing is said. I make a joke about it, and they fucking sell it to the tabloids. Anything to get the magazine some press. And that's really sad.

'Ever since that article I've been known as "Lily Allen, pint-sized potty-mouth pop star who once admitted she would celebrate her No. 1 single by taking cocaine!" Now I have read many articles in the *NME*, where male band members freely admit to, or associate themselves with the taking of drugs, and I haven't seen many of them ending up in the tabloids. Take the Klaxons, for example, and the ongoing MDMA [ecstasy] references. "MDMAZING" I believe was the title of a recent article – how responsible!

'The thing I find funny about that is you get

journalists saying, "Lily is such an irresponsible role model." But hang on, you're the people lying about what I am. Maybe you should be taking some responsibility for the image of me you're portraying to young people to try to sell papers. Stop trying to attack me for something I haven't done. The only people it affects in my eyes are the kids, and there's nothing I can do about how they're going to twist my words.'

It seemed that Lily was being punished for the exact same reason she was being celebrated a few weeks earlier. She was a young girl with forthright views, honest about her background and saying what she believed in, unlike most modern pop stars, who are media-trained to be bland and vague in interviews. It would have been foolish to want to lose such a strong part of Lily's appeal.

Thankfully, she refused to be silenced and would continue to say what she felt, damning the consequences – albeit with a more hardened awareness of the media. 'I thought that if I was just honest and said, "Yeah, I've taken drugs and I have sex and like a drink", then no one would be able to write "Lily Allen in Cocaine Shocker", but they still manage to do it.

'I'm a jokey person, I don't say everything seriously

but that doesn't come across in print very well. And maybe I have to be aware of that, but I'm definitely not going to start keeping my opinions to myself because that's not me. I was only joking about the gak, but then I read in the *NME* that I do this and that, whereas Pete Doherty, he's cool!'

It wasn't to be her first run-in with *NME*. When the music magazine announced their annual Cool List for 2006, Lily was one of five girls to make it into the Top Ten. In a male-dominated industry this was a turn-up for the books and something of a milestone. To celebrate, the magazine asked the five ladies, Beth Ditto from the Gossip, Lovefoxxx of Canser de Sei Sexy, Kate Jackson from the Long Blondes, Karen O from the Yeah Yeah Yeahs and Lily, to pose on the cover.

'I vowed not to work with them again, but as the context was so important, i.e. a strong female presence in music, I thought I might as well put aside my differences and do it. Now I don't care for the Cool List, and I said this to them in the interview. I don't really think the *NME* are in any position to tell us who is cool and who isn't. Personally I don't think a bunch of people sitting in an office drinking tea, inventing musical genres, and watching Nathan Barley DVDs are leading any kind of cool brigade, do you? But I did find it interesting that they wanted to put five women on the cover, and wanted to name 2006 our year.'

However, Lily got a surprise when she went and picked up a copy of the magazine and found that instead of a cover championing the girls, as promised, they replaced them with 'another fucking Muse cover. I like Muse, in fact *Black Holes and Revelations* is one of my favourite albums of this year. But the *NME* have covered them so much this year already.'

Lily was also furious that she did not receive a courtesy call to inform her that she was being pulled off the cover, and she was seething when she read editor Conor McNicholas's press release. He stated 'From Beth to Lily to Karen, they've brought new energy to a scene dominated by men. They're also living proof that you can still rock a crowd when you're wearing stilettos.'

As you can imagine, Lily wasn't impressed. 'I mean, how fucking patronising. "You can still rock a crowd wearing stilettos." Is that all we are, stiletto-wearing people? Is that all he could say that we brought? Don't make me sick, we've always been here, you arrogant prick. This was your chance to actually show you meant it. And instead you put

Muse on the cover. Because you thought that your readers might not buy a magazine with an overweight lesbian [Beth] and a not particularly attractive-looking me on the front. Wankers .You should take your heads out of your New Rave arses, and actually think about your responsibilities to youth culture, and to women in general.'

Beth Ditto from the Gossip agreed with Lily's opinion. 'They totally copped out. I think it's disappointing because I actually thought that things were getting somewhere, and they were just too chicken. I think it's just another weird, backhanded gesture towards women in the music industry. And had they all been men, I'm sure it would have made it on the cover.'

Lily still wasn't finished with the subject, adding, 'It was a bit wimpish of them. And the women who work in that office – to let that happen! That's the sort of things that happen in the media and those things aren't going to change unless someone like me says something about it occasionally.'

It wouldn't be long before a whole host of celebrities would similarly find themselves on the receiving of Lily's acid tongue.

This 'self-conscious' girl with a 'lack of self-esteem' finally had the platform she had always craved, and it wouldn't be long before her music was suddenly pushed into the background as she delivered one barbed comment after another. And it didn't take the press long either to recognise Lily's value. Put a Dictaphone in front of her, quiz her about a few of her peers and wait for the ready-made headline spinner.

Lily was more than happy to oblige. The Dirty Pretty Things' frontman Carl Barat, the Kooks' Luke Pritchard and British guitar music in general were all slammed by her, as she accused them of thinking they are above their fans.

'You'd think that people in bands would be happy. They don't have to sit in an office all day sweating in this blistering heat. Well, you'd be wrong. Carl Barat is obviously convinced he's God or something. Carl didn't make eye contact with anyone and they have organic sliced bread on the rider. I went to school with Luke from the Kooks. I thought he was cool then. I was quite annoyed at how much of a bad man he thinks he is. There is no excuse for wearing broken straw hats and dark sunglasses two storeys underground at Alexandra Palace. Boys, your regurgitated indie rock days are over, so get over yourselves.'

She also blasted Victoria Beckham, saying, 'I don't

care how much she says that's her natural weight, it's bull. She gets photographed every day and doesn't eat a thing' – and had a televised ruckus on BBC comedy show *Never Mind the Buzzcocks* with pop star Jamelia. Lily was annoyed that Jamelia had asked her record company for a specially made child-friendly copy of the hit album *Alright, Still* for her young daughter Teja.

'Teja's really into Lily's singles so I'm getting a clean album, only for personal purposes. It's a perk of being on the same label. I think Lily's wicked. She's enjoying being young and it's refreshing. It would be lovely if she didn't change but there are some things on the album not suitable for young kids,' Jamelia explained.

Lily wasn't happy and made Jamelia aware of it: 'I'm not being funny, Jamelia, but I never made my album for your child. Besides, I think children should have some swearing. It's good for them.'

Lily even found time to launch a foul-mouthed rant at Sir Bob Geldof, calling him a 'cunt' and insisting he is 'so self-important and takes himself far too seriously. I'm just not a fan at all.'

That is something she has in common with her dad, who says, 'I hate Bob Geldof more than any person living on the planet, to be honest. I've loathed him since at least 1985 [Live Aid]. Don't get me wrong – I think the awareness stuff is brilliant but people themselves can be "the personality". We don't need figureheads.'

And as for Sir Bob Geldof's daughter Peaches, well, that was a long-running feud with Lily. When Lily was asked who she hated, she replied, 'Peaches Geldof. Because of who she is. I find it really offensive, like she did this, like, documentary about Islam and it was really awful. I watched it on *Richard and Judy* and it was like, "Yeah, I just really think that kids in this country don't really know enough about Islam and I think that they just really need to know a lot more about Islam." What do you know about Islam, you useless oaf?' When asked if she'd fight her, Allen replied, "Yep, I would kick her over, then kick her even harder when she was down. I would probably, like, stamp on my can of Magners and then stab her in the ear."

Paris Hilton was next, with Lily taking offence that the socialite was releasing an album. 'Paris is hideously untalented. I poured my heart into my album. She just got someone else to do it for her. If she's rude to me I'll punch her.

'Five years ago Paris Hilton's album would have done really well over here because we didn't have things like the internet, we didn't have bands like myself or Arctic Monkeys. Now people can see her for what she is, and think, Go away! What makes you think you have a life? Paris Hilton's album did really badly over here and I just think it's so boring and pathetic and it shouldn't happen. It's the fucking record companies that sign things like that, and you think, What are you doing? Why are you ruining your own job? It's just laziness. People cheesy enough to buy albums like that should be killed.'

It's a subject she takes seriously. She detests manufactured, soulless music. 'I take all my lyrical inspiration from my recent life. Every song on my album is a snapshot of a certain moment. I find it really pathetic when you're watching TV interviews with shit bands like the Pussycat Dolls and someone asks, "What's this song about' and they're like, "Well, you know, it's kind of like that feeling you get when…" I'm like, "You didn't even write it – shut up."'

But she feels the current trend of guitar music is just as bad. 'I like lots of indie bands. I'm a fan of good guitar music. I think it's just that at the moment everyone's like, "Music's so great, we've got these great indie rock bands." But in reality they all sound the same. They're just doing what S Club 7 and Steps did – regurgitating the same songs because that's what people are buying at the moment.'

But it wouldn't be long before people started to bite back. Carl Barat remained unperturbed by her rant at him, laughing, 'Sometimes you meet people you're captivated by and others you're not interested in. She was one of them. It's like getting slagged off by Jade Goody.'

Others waded in, including Melanie Blatt from the re-formed girl band All Saints, who accused Lily, during an interview with the magazine *Attitude*, of picking on people who are 'soft targets', adding, 'I think she picks on the wrong people, to be honest. I think there's a certain type of person you're allowed to pick on, but she always goes for the weak and I don't like that.' Former Mis-Teeq MC Alesha Harvey agreed, warning the singer, 'I don't like hearing her putting down other artists – we should all support each other. It's wrong to do it as it can mislead the public.'

Even David Beckham stepped in, claiming he refused to even listen to her music after her series of disparaging comments aimed at his wife. 'She was horrible to Victoria, so I won't have that.'

But Lily finally got what she wanted when rapper Lady Sovereign stepped into the ring for a series of funny, if lightweight, feuds. She first denounced Lily's title of the Queen of MySpace, claiming she was the true heir, before calling her 'the biggest chav going' and said the pop star was only famous because of her dad.

Lily snapped back, 'Everyone is so obsessed with celebrity culture that they presume that because my dad has been in a couple of B-movies and wrote some shit football song, I've been driving around in limos all my life. This connections thing is such bullshit. As if my dad just rings someone up in Parlophone and says, "Lily hasn't got a job right now, can you give her a record deal?" "Yeah, sure, Keith, 'cos you've got such a good reputation and you're so hard-working."

'In response to Miss Sovereign's comments, I've spoken to my dad and he says he's happy to adopt you if you think it will give you a leg up.'

Lily saved her biggest and most controversial battle until last. Unsurprisingly, given her history of not responding well to authority, she refused to adhere to pop protocol and instead did something no other mainstream girl act has ever done and blasted Madonna – calling her 'irrelevant'.

Talking in the August 2006 British edition of *GQ* magazine, Lily ranted, 'I haven't got anything against her at all but she hasn't done anything since the early eighties that has been, like, "wow". She might have meant something once but I don't know anyone my age who cares.'

The press had a field day. How dare this upstart newcomer take on the Queen of Pop?

Since exploding into the music charts in 1983 with the hit single 'Holiday', Madonna has changed the face of pop music with an astonishing number of hits and successful reinventions. As such, it's a given that every female pop act after her should and would acknowledge Madonna accordingly – never more so than in the extraordinary display at the 2003 MTV Video Music Awards, when Britney Spears and Christina Aguilera shocked viewers by passionately kissing the pop queen.

But times were changing and Lily the loud-mouthed pop pixie was at the forefront of new musical climate – where the power of individual personality had never been higher.

Nevertheless, as with the 'gak' comment, Lily was quick to embark on a damage-limitation exercise – once she had assessed the public reaction. She admitted, 'They'll say, "Who is the most overrated person in pop in your opinion?" And I'll say, "Well, maybe Madonna", and all of a sudden it's like, Lily hates Madonna! I guess with it all happening so quickly I haven't figured out how it all works yet.'

She now realises that 'sarcasm is the lowest form of wit, I know, and it also doesn't read very well. I shall not be talking in a sarcastic tone for a while.'

However, it's doubtful if Lily will keep to her new promise. There is no evidence from her life so far that she will ever stop saying what she feels whenever and wherever she wants.

CHAPTER FOURTEEN

ALRIGHT, STILL

'I started to feel like I could have a voice. But I wanted to write about my own world in an entertaining way. So I did.'

The public couldn't wait to get their hands on Lily's debut album: 17 July 2006 couldn't have come fast enough. They were lucky to get it that soon. January 2007 was the original planned date, and who knows how things would have ended up with five extra months of editing and re-recording.

Made completely on Lily's terms, the album was a smash. And she knew she had made it because straight away she started getting grief from the people she sings about on the record.

'Well, I wrote all those before anyone knew who I was. I was just kind of making the songs for myself and a few other people. So now it occurs to me but at the time it didn't. Anyway, the majority of the songs on the album are about my fucking ex-boyfriends who broke up with me, so I don't care about how they feel about them. I can't bite my tongue. It's just not in me. And it does get me into countless bits of trouble.

'When I made that song about Alfie no one knew who I was. I was just writing songs about my life. Alfie will get back at me, don't you worry. I have learned that speaking about my family upsets them, so I'm not going to do it any more.'

At Lily's album launch party, the star of the show was dressed in trademark ball gown, happily mingling with label mates and members of the press. She looked amazing and had already developed a remarkable stage presence that belied her small frame. She may have been relatively new to the fame game but Lily looked as if she owned the night. And she did: they were all there for her.

All her toil and hardship – writing down lyrics to beats, raking through record collections, finding the right influences and samples and engaging in long discussions with her producers and collaborators to decide what worked and what didn't – had finally paid off.

It was a lavish event and a far cry from that day in September 2005 when she first signed her 'really,

really small development deal' at the record label for £25,000. The label had no idea the young singer they were looking at would be their big success story. As Lily remembered it, 'At that time they were putting out a Kylie album, a Coldplay album, the Gorillaz album had just been released. So, they didn't really care about me.'

They did now, and Lily was having a ball. Hollywood actress Keira Knightley came to the event to support her new pal with Lily's brother Alfie. Lily wasn't the only one in the Allen-Owen family starting to make a name for themselves. Alfie was becoming a respected actor and he and Keira were now co-stars in the film *Atonement*, based on Ian McEwan's bestselling novel.

As the night got merry, so did Lily. She made her way to the outdoor party, her fabulous dress slithering through the mud as she messily climbed on stage to grab the microphone while managing to drunkenly slur the words 'Happy Birthday' to a partygoer. It was a successful and memorable night for Lily, and one of many to come, because her debut album was a staggering accomplishment.

Alright, Still tells a story. Reading the lyrics from each song is like sitting in on a therapy session with the singer herself and it's clear Lily unburdened a great deal of her stresses, anger and frustrations when writing it. The title itself, taken from a lyric in the track 'Knock 'Em Out', suggests she has survived intact and strong, despite the struggles and strains her life has presented her with.

In the course of the journey the album takes the listener on, we get to learn about her love life, family life, her insecurities and the difficulties of growing up a girl in an image-obsessed world.

'SMILE'

The first track on the album, 'Smile', was Lily's debut single and the song most people associate with her, even now.

She sings about her anger towards a cheating boyfriend she found out was 'fucking the girl next door'. She describes how the hurt and frustration and longing turned into anger and bitterness and a thirst for revenge. From loneliness to action and satisfaction, Lily struck a chord with many a wronged girlfriend, to find light at the end of the tunnel.

When the tables turned and the cheating ex began to regret his actions, Lily was left with the upper hand and, through her hurt, began to take joy from his pain.

The lyrics suggest Lily was heavily influenced by

her relationship with early love, DJ Lester Lloyd – and the video removes any shadow of doubt. In it a DJ character is cast as the protagonist, whom she routinely tortures by arranging for him to be beaten up, poisoned with laxatives and his flat ransacked and records ruined, while she looks on and smiles.

Lloyd claims he didn't cheat on Lily, and Lily has never admitted a link between the character in the song and her ex. But there is clearly a connection.

The track itself is an upbeat and bouncy song, written by Lily and Future Cut and built on a sunny sample from the Soul Brothers' 1960s classic 'Free Soul'. Indeed, when it was first aired on the radio, many listeners failed to look beyond the happy sound, failing to notice the darker message. It would soon become a theme for Lily's songs, with deeper truths hiding beneath a soft and accessible shell.

'KNOCK 'EM OUT'

Girl power for the 21st century, 'Knock 'Em Out' portrays a more truthful account of life as a teenage girl than the Spice Girls ever managed.

Lily says of the song: 'It's about being chatted up by annoying guys. I don't know what guys expect when they shout something at you and then drive away. Do they expect you to scream "stop, come back"? There is a certain manoeuvre at a bar situation where you bang the top of their nose with your fist when it comes down. It doesn't hurt that much but it makes their eyes water so it looks like they're crying really quickly.'

Lily sounds startlingly self-assured and aware of the weaknesses of the opposite sex.

'Knock 'Em Out' is a Mike Skinner-esque call-to-arms for all girls to fight back against sexually predatory men who won't take no for an answer when trying to chat them up.

'LDN'

The second single released from *Alright, Still*, 'LDN' tackled darker depths than 'Smile' – again hiding a disturbing meaning behind Lily's cheerful bubblegum-pop sound.

We hear her describe a bicycle ride through London. Lily's unable to drive because the police have taken away her licence – a reference to her drink-driving conviction. And soon the London she describes turns from one of happiness and joy to a gloomy observation of the city's darker side. She sings about mugging and seedy sex.

Throughout the song – and its accompanying video – we are taken on a trip through London and shown what there is to see behind the shadows.

The lyrics display considerable maturity, and highlight Lily's vision of the world. Her often difficult childhood forced her to grow up quickly and confront life's uncomfortable truths earlier than most girls her age.

Nevertheless, Lily clearly loves London for all its faults.

'EVERYTHING'S JUST WONDERFUL'

The fourth track on the album addresses issues more personal to Lily and gives us an insight into her deepest thoughts, concerns and insecurities.

Behind the upbeat reggae-ska sound, the lyrics describe how she pretends all is well, when in reality her mind is beset with issues. She talks of money worries and of her desire to be a healthy and natural role model.

'NOT BIG'

If 'Everything's Just Wonderful' shows a defiant but softer side to Lily Allen, she brings out her arsenal in 'Not Big'.

The song – with a dancehall sound – begins with a

hard-faced Lily talking at the end of a relationship. After being dumped she tells the man he never satisfied her sexually and she had to take drugs to have fun with him. She then threatens to sleep with his friends.

The song is riddled with sexual put-downs and the lyrics suggest it is about her relationship with Lester Lloyd, which lasted 18 months, picking up where 'Smile' left off. But Lily insists it's about no one in particular and points out that more than one of her ex-boyfriends believe it's about them.

She says, 'The girl teases him about his knob. All girls do, talk behind their back when they split up about their knobs. Sorry, boys, but it's true. Be afraid.'

'FRIDAY NIGHT'

As the album continues, so does the therapy session with Lily – and 'Friday Night' is no exception. She paints a picture of a Friday night out with girlfriends and describes run-ins with clubbers and catty encounters with other girls.

Lily has often described how she gets on better with boys than girls and this song describes her disdain for mouthy and aggressive girls in nightclubs, singing about a night out where things get heated between her and a girl on a guest list.

'SHAME FOR YOU'

Lily switches her attention from competitive girls back to cheating men in 'Shame For You' and the claws are out again for another philandering beau.

She describes discovering the boyfriend's indiscretion and confronting him with plenty of girl power. But Lily reminds us she's still a girl reliant on her brother Alfie and stepbrother Kevin.

'LITTLEST THINGS'

'Littlest Things' stands out from other tracks on the album because it's a ballad. Lily hangs up her anger for a softer, gentler mood. She reminisces about a lost love, but in a melancholy way. Remembering this lost love, she asks if it can't be patched up. Lily tells a bittersweet tale about how, after a relationship has come and gone, it's easy to remember the little things that made it work, while ignoring the reasons the relationship ended.

She wrote the song after splitting up with Seb Chew, and it promptly inspired them to get back together after he constantly listened to it.

'TAKE WHAT YOU WANT'

Lily rails against an unwanted influence again in 'Take What You Want', an upbeat, poppy track. It's not clear if it's her father, mother or older boyfriend Seb who is the object of her attention.

She sings of her desire to live her own life and make her own decisions despite being younger and having fewer experiences. Lily later revealed she didn't like the track and disapproved of its inclusion on the album. She wanted B-sides 'Cheryl Tweedy' or 'Absolutely Nothing' to take its place. But the record company put its foot down. 'I fucking hate that song more than anything in the world,' said Lily. 'They [the record company] said the Robbie Williams market would like it.'

'FRIEND OF MINE'

A mellow reggae-inspired track, 'Friend Of Mine' expresses Lily's disdain for boring friends who need drugs to maintain a personality. The song reflects Lily's frustration – dating back to her school days – at her inability to relate to other girls of her age, her feeling older and at a different stage in her life.

'ALFIE'

Capping the album off, 'Alfie' reminds the listener of what Lily does best – pop with attitude. In this bubblegum, cartoon track, Lily urges her brother Alfie to stop smoking weed and to pull his life together. The colourful video makes the song, but the catchy and addictive pop-ska tune, written by Lily and Greg Kursten, and laugh-along lyrics make it impossible to avoid humming along to. The song is even more amusing to anyone who has met Lily's brother Alfie Owen-Allen. Friends claim the song sums up her younger sibling perfectly.

Shy Alfie refused to appear in the video – and was replaced by a puppet!

CHAPTER FIFTEEN

LILY ON SCREEN

'Being comfortable is being confident, and being confident is good'

Lily's look was perfect for the music video and great care was taken to capture the mood of her songs when it came to recreating them on the small screen.

Sophie Muller was chosen to direct the video for Lily's first single, 'Smile'. Muller came with a pedigree, having made the upbeat promo for Shakira's hit 'Hips Don't Lie'. And the story she told perfectly suited 'Smile', with its hidden swipe at Lily's ex-boyfriend DJ Lester Lloyd.

Lily's lyrics castigate a DJ ex for sleeping with the girl next door, before adding how pleased she is to see his suffering.

In the video Lily is shown getting revenge on the ex by paying a gang of thugs to beat him up. As she takes him to a cafe to console him, the thugs ransack his home and scratch his records. Meanwhile at the cafe, a conniving Lily laces his drink with laxatives, so when he returns home to discover his home trashed, he also suffers a bout of diarrhoea. At the end of the video, Lily is seen smiling as the ex discovers the damage to his discs while he's DJ-ing at a club.

The video landed Lily in trouble with TV watchdog Ofcom, because it contained the word 'fucking', showed a mugging, a violent burglary and the spiking of a drink. It was banned from being shown at a time when children might watch and edited to remove the swearing. Fearful of a fine, MTV pulled the promo from its schedules altogether. Lily insists she was more offended than any viewers may have been: 'I got really offended when my single, "Smile", got banned from MTV in the UK because it had the word "fuck" in it. Yet the Pussycat Dolls can get away with gyrating with no clothes on and promoting prostitution.'

The controversy wasn't necessarily a bad thing for Lily. She had burst on to the scene in a spectacular way – and a talked-about video helped keep up the momentum.

Two versions were made of Lily's second video,

which was to accompany the single 'LDN'. The first was a hastily made promo to accompany the seven-inch special release of the track. The speeded-up film showed Lily zipping through London ('LDN' is text-speak for London) on a chopper bicycle. It was so low-budget she is filmed leaving the very north London house she still shares with her mother and brother before making her way to Primrose Hill and on to Ladbroke Grove tube station. She gets off the underground and cycles around Buckingham Palace and along the Thames riverside.

The film shows the simple pleasures of life in London, and presents Lily as a young, approachable and accessible character. It was important at the time for her to remain the character her fans discovered on MySpace – someone young and carefree, like they were.

When the single was re-released in September 2006, there was more time and money to reflect the lyrics and present a side to the song that the casual listen may not have picked up on.

Nima Nizouradeh – who had created promos for Hot Chip and Jamie T – was recruited to direct what would be a thought-provoking video. At the beginning of the video, before the music kicks in, Lily enters a music shop, where she asks two members of staff, 'Have you got any punky, electronica, grime, new wave grime, like broken beats? Dubby broken beats, kinda like soulful. Like drum'n'bass, but broken drum'n'bass?' When the staff members tell her no such thing exists, Lily leaves and makes a date to meet someone. The stand-out scenes appears to show her boasting that her music is unique and crosses musical boundaries in a way no other artist's has. The terms Lily uses are all words that had been used by journalists in attempting to describe her music.

After leaving the record shop, Lily embarks on the journey described in the song, in which she discovers London isn't the happy place she first thought. The point is summed up in the chorus, urging people to look beyond the surface, which often conceals the truth.

As she passes through London we see it turn from a bright, sunny place into a dark and gloomy city and the scenes portrayed change from good to bad. Two figures in a doorway become a pimp and prostitute; a Romeo and Juliet scene becomes a woman throwing her partner's belongings out of a window; two men eating lunch on a bench become tramps; a magician's wand becomes a rusted nail; and a sweet becomes a cigarette butt. At the very end of the video, Lily takes another call, cancelling the date she has arranged, and storms off unhappy, leaving a dank and grey London behind her.

The arresting video will have shocked many who presumed the cheery and upbeat song had a happy message. It showed Lily was an artist determined that her videos had message and meaning.

Lily's next assault on the video scene, for 'Littlest Things', would present her in a more glamorous light – and give her the chance to travel back to an era that influenced her image profoundly, the 1950s.

This time Lily traded her ball gown and bubblegum look for an Audrey Hepburn style, complete with tied-back hair and mackintosh. The song, a ballad, was a dramatic departure from the other tracks on her album, and the video reflected that. Beautifully shot in black and white, Lily is whisked off her feet by a Humphrey Bogart-like protagonist shown only in silhouette form. The cinematic film is clearly influenced by director Douglas Sirk's melodramas of the 1950s. It is her most grown-up video and marks a clear transition from Lily Allen the accidental pop star to Lily Allen the music icon.

But fans of the traditional Lily look had no need to fear – the bubblegum was back in time for the next single, in a big way.

'Alfie' is about Lily's little brother and in the song she tells him off for locking himself in his bedroom, smoking cannabis, playing computer games, reading porn and masturbating. In the cartoony video Alfie is recreated as a grotesque puppet, while Lily is a 1950s housewife, scolding him for 'wasting his life away'.

Plans for the video changed a lot from the original storyboard. Alfie was meant to play himself – but he refused, fearful of being mocked in the song and on screen. So a puppet likeness was created. The plan then was to have his puppet as the star and a stand-in for Lily. In the end she stepped in and played herself – desperate not to be left out of the fun.

The video was directed by Sarah Chatfield, who used some of her childhood friends as inspiration – with a bit of Tom and Jerry chucked in for good measure. She explains, 'I always had this soft spot for Tom and Jerry. In their cartoons there's always this human character cut off at the waist. So I was going to have someone stand in for Lily and we would just show the bottom of the feet or her trainers and have this character interact with the puppets this way. It was in a later stage that it was decided we would have Lily in the video. When I listened to the track, it struck me how much it sounded like a cartoon. I could just see bright colours all over. I wanted to create a slightly musical feel to the whole production. Like the way Snow White has birds and animals around her. That old Disney touch: something good fun and cartoon-like.'

CHAPTER SIXTEEN

WINNING OVER THE CRITICS

'She never sounds like she's trying too hard.'
ROLLING STONE MAGAZINE

Few debut albums win over music critics as unanimously as Lily's did. Journalists united in their praise of *Alright, Still* and this, coupled with public approval, helped it to No. 2 in the UK album charts after its release. Although it was unable to shift Razorlight's eponymous second album from the top spot, it was quite an achievement for a first effort – *Alright, Still* was the 29th-bestselling album of 2006, with 523,000 copies sold – and the critics were impressed.

British music bible *NME* was among the first to offer Lily praise, reviewer Priya Elan heralding pop's newest bright young thing and giving *Alright, Still* seven out of ten: 'Lily Allen is like the perfect modern pop star. She's the photogenic, self-styled Queen of Blogs with quips a-go-go. She's an unrelenting, media untrained 21-year-old whose blog is like an unbovvered raspberry in the face of celebrity. With a personality this size, this isn't the last time you'll be hearing from her.'

There was more gushing backslapping to come from the British broadsheets – notoriously tough nuts to crack. Both the *Observer Music Monthly*'s Rosie Swash and the *Guardian*'s Sophie Heawood offered Lily maximum points. Swash warned: 'Lily Allen faces a daunting mission crossing over from the blogosphere to the charts.' But she rightly predicted Lily's success: 'Her cocksure debut album *Alright, Still* justifies the hype. Drawing on everything from the soft-core reggae of "Friday Night" to the fairground pomp of "Alfie", Allen has fused together a uniquely acidic brand of pop, and the icing on the cake is that brutally barbed tongue. "Don't take me on…" she warns a potential nemesis on the languidly malevolent "Shame for You". As if we'd dare.'

Heawood said, 'If the album is rough round the edges, that amateurism serves to bring the listener in; makes you feel like you're in a conversation with your best mate. The female Mike Skinner? She's far, far better than that.'

The great reviews just kept coming in. John Lewis from *Time Out* in Lily's native London gave it a resounding five out of six and offered a brief but concise endorsement: 'Her debut album is actually rather fantastic.'

Not everyone was won over, but it seemed the reserved reviews came from critics unsure whether Lily could translate originality into chart success. Chris Cottingham from music magazine *Q* gave *Alright, Still* three out of five. He was impressed but his review had a sting in the tail. 'Her debut album is poised to be the soundtrack of the summer. The lilting skank of first single "Smile" burns itself deep into your brain, "LDN"'s brass parps have an instantly. The overall effect is not too dissimilar to Sugababes, only with added adult content.'

Comparison to pop trio Sugababes wouldn't have pleased Lily, but in general the reviews were excellent, and besides, she was too busy appearing on TV, radio and performing to promote *Alright, Still*, to dwell on the thoughts of the critics.

The album was one of the success stories of 2006, but with 2007 came new challenges, and her label, Regal, was pushing her to dip her feet in the American music market.

The US has always been the musical Holy Grail for British artists. So many have tried and so few have succeeded. In the past ten years, new acts from the UK to have made any real impact across the Atlantic can be counted on one hand. But EMI was confident that Lily's original sound would suit a changing US market and set out as early as October 2006 to test the water. After a few gigs to establish her name among those in the know, Lily returned in January 2007 to release *Alright, Still* to an anticipating American market. And they loved her even more than the British did.

She charmed the socks off even the most discerning US music critics. *Rolling Stone*'s Rob Sheffield offered a generous seven out of ten and said, 'The 21-year-old London brat writes shambling pop songs, rooted in ska and rap, with cheeky rhymes – she never sounds like she's trying too hard.'

Blender magazine gave it nine out of ten, gushing, 'What's amazing about *Alright, Still* is how similar the girl with the blog is to the girl with the hit record.' Dubbing it 'All gleam with upmarket panache', the valued opinion-makers at *Spin* magazine afforded Lily's efforts eight out of ten.

The *Austin Chronicle* in Texas, where Lily would go on to impress at the South by Southwest festival in March 2007, was equally won over. Giving the album four out of five, reviewer Dan Oko said: 'Like Blondie circa 1981, Allen breathes needed fresh air into the game, and the fact that she spends most of her time dissing ex-boyfriends just shows that sometimes writing what you know remains a viable musical strategy. Adding to her favor, Allen spits side-splitting insults worthy of Eminem's heyday.'

And it wasn't just Lily's album that had Americans on their feet and dancing. She could hold her own live. The weighty *Washington Post* caught Lily at a gig to promote the album in February 2007 and posed the incredibly complimentary question, 'Can a Grammy nomination for best new artist be far behind?'

It wasn't to be in 2007 – but it was clear from the media appraisal of *Alright, Still* that Lily had made a lasting impression on the people that count across the pond, and gone where Robbie Williams and Westlife dared to tread and failed.

The icing on the American cake was an endorsement from cultural barometer Hollywood-based online gossip columnist Perez Hilton, who embraced Lily and her album with open arms. He wrote: 'We are thankful for Lily Allen's outspokenness! As if her music weren't fresh enough, her candour in interviews is even more refreshing.'

CHAPTER SEVENTEEN

THE HITS OF ALRIGHT, STILL

> 'Every song on my album is a snapshot of a certain moment.'

'Smile' entered the UK singles chart on Sunday 2 July 2006 in 13th position – on internet downloads alone. It was an impressive start and Lily wouldn't have to wait long for the No. 1 she so craved. Another week of promotional work and radio play was all it needed to propel the track to the top spot, replacing Shakira and Wyclef Jean's summer smash hit 'Hips Don't Lie'.

Seven days later 'Smile' held off Shakira and Wyclef and a strong challenge from the Rogue Traders' 'Voodoo Child' and Nelly Furtado's

'Maneater' to stay in prime position for a second week. It eventually slipped to fourth spot in its third week in the charts, replaced by McFly's Sport Relief charity single 'Don't Stop Me Now/Please Please'.

After an impressive seven weeks in the Top Ten, 'Smile' dropped out – but stayed in the Top Forty for an incredible 21 weeks. In fact it was still kicking around, at No. 52, in January 2007, a whole six months after it was released.

'Smile' was one of the big hits of 2006 – selling 228,500 copies, earning Lily a shiny silver disc and finishing 11th in a list of the year's top tracks. The names of the artists ahead of her show how much Lily achieved with her first release. She was now in the company of Gnarls Barkley, Shakira, the Scissor Sisters, Nelly Furtado, Take That and Justin Timberlake. Lily was in fine company.

'Smile' wasn't just a hit in Lily's native UK – she made a splash all over the world. She reached No. 1 in Poland; 6 in Ireland and New Zealand; 10 in the Netherlands; 14 in Australia; 16 in France; 21 in Switzerland; 27 in Belgium, 38 in Sweden; 39 in Austria, 61 in Germany; and 69 as far afield as Mexico.

Keen to follow up the success of the single, Regal pushed forward the release of her debut album *Alright, Still*. It was released on 17 July and entered the album chart on Sunday 23 July at No. 2. It was a staggering achievement. The LP was released on the same day as Razorlight's eponymous second album and Scottish crooner Paolo Nutini's much-hyped debut. Lily beat Nutini and came in at an admirable second place behind Razorlight, whose first album had helped them build up an unassailable fan base. Lily's album outsold the Kooks' debut, as well as celebrated acts Muse and Snow Patrol.

After a strong second week of release, *Alright, Still* only slipped one place to No. 3, behind Razorlight and Snow Patrol. It fell out of the Top Ten on 20 August, after an impressive four weeks – only to return following the release of follow-up singles 'LDN', 'Littlest Things' and 'Alfie'. All in all, *Alright, Still* enjoyed ten weeks in the Top Ten. The album won Lily a gold disc on 21 July 2006, after just four days on sale; and a platinum disc two months later, on 15 September, when it passed 400,000 sales. By December *Alright, Still* had made it into the list of 2006's bestselling albums, in 29th place, having sold more than 523,000 copies in the UK.

In March 2007, after 26 weeks on sale, *Alright, Still* was still in the 28th slot in the UK album chart, ahead of the Scissor Sisters, David Bowie and a new release from Neil Young.

Unsurprisingly, the album also made an impact outside the UK. It reached a high of sixth place in the Irish album chart, No. 7 in Australia, 21 in Canada, 22 in New Zealand and 37 in Japan. Most impressive is America's response to Lily. At the time of going to print, *Alright, Still* reached a peak of 20 in the notoriously tough-to-crack US Billboard Album Chart.

Two months after the album came out, in September 2006, Lily released 'LDN', the second single from it. A single released after the album was less likely to trouble the charts, because most of her hardcore fans would already have a copy of the song, but 'LDN' still peaked at No. 6 after its second week on sale, and managed six weeks in the Top Forty. The Top Ten at the time of its release was dominated by the Scissor Sisters' hit 'I Don't Feel Like Dancin'', The Killers' 'When You Were Young' and Justin Timberlake's 'Sexy Back' – so there was no shame in sixth spot.

'LDN', which was first released by Lily on seven-inch vinyl in April 2007, also continued the singer's assault on the world charts, making the Top Ten in Australia, Ireland, New Zealand, Poland and Switzerland.

Lily's fans had to wait another three months for the next single, the ballad 'Littlest Things', which struggled to make an impact in the charts. It peaked at No. 21, never troubling Take That and X Factor winner Leona Lewis, who made the top spot their own in December with their singles 'Patience' and 'A Moment Like This'.

The song, a ballad unlike anything else Lily's fans were likely to have heard, was only released in the UK, on downloads and in Poland, where it reached No. 37. Back home, it disappeared without trace after seven weeks in the charts, last being seen in the depths at No. 67.

The bubblegum pop of 'Alfie' – a plea to her layabout brother – performed much better. It only reached the heights of No. 15 in the UK and reminded her fans that Lily was still alive and kicking, at a time when she was busy travelling the world showing off her music to audiences in the US, as well as putting the finishing touches to the clothing designs for her forthcoming collection with New Look. Alas neither Lily's loyal fan base in Poland nor anyone else in the world got the chance to get their hands on a copy of the 'Alfie' single. It was released only in the UK.

Nevertheless, album sales were strong and figures suggested new fans were going out and buying Lily's album rather than the singles. Besides, she was too busy planning for the future to worry about the performance of her singles. And anyway, there was another single planned for release in February that would remind her fans of the real Lily.

CHAPTER EIGHTEEN

THE LILY LOOK

'If I didn't work in music, I'd work in fashion in some way.'

On a wet night on 4 October 2006, fans of Lily descended upon Porchester Hall in west London to see the petite pop star perform. She hadn't even released a single until a few months before but was quickly becoming a household name – and soaking-wet girls were everywhere, wringing newly acquired Lily-style ball gowns dry and squelching Nike trainers through puddle after puddle.

'There were about a hundred girls all dressed up as Lily,' remarked journalist Sarah Henshaw, who was covering the event. 'I like Lily's music but I didn't realise the impact she had on young girls. They were all about 16 and 17 years old and they were absolutely obsessed with her. I went into the bathroom just before Lily came on and it was like that scene in the Hitchcock film *The Birds* where the heroes have to creep to their car while tiptoeing past an army of birds who are just sitting there watching them. It was like that in the bathroom, but instead of feathers, it was lacy sequined gowns I walked past. The bathroom was full of Lily clones.'

Lilymania was starting to take hold. She was the perfect pop package. She had the catchy ska-like songs, the talent, the brains and, more importantly, she had a defining look. It's one that has exploded; from a smattering of hardcore fans imitating their role model to high-street shoppers taking crumpled magazine pictures of Lily out of their handbags while they scour the shops to replicate their new favourite look.

You can now log on to eBay and get dresses in the style of Lily Allen. 'There was one group who flew all the way over from Texas just for one night to see me,' she recalls. 'They were called the Lilettes, and they were all wearing clothes like mine. I met them briefly. It was really flattering. I told my mum and she was like, "Oh my God, that's so sweet, well, you should let them stay here" and I was like "You what?" I'm scared of going home in case my mum meets random fans and brings them home for a cup of tea.'

Like her music, her look was one of contradictions. Take a ball gown, add plenty of mismatched jewellery, throw a pair of hoop earrings on, slip on some Nike trainers, and voila – you have an image that grabbed hold of 2006, shook the boho out of its system and wrapped it up in a blend of chav couture and American high-school prom.

There was also an element of family heritage to her image. 'I wear lots of gold jewellery because I like it, but also because my dad's mother was a Romany gypsy, so it's kind of tradition. I'm a middle-class girl from London.'

She has come a long way from the scruffy-looking schoolkid with messed-up hair and grungy clothes who would shuffle through class. Her new style has won admiration from a host of fashion icons including Chanel designer Karl Lagerfeld – and little wonder, considering *Grazia* magazine hailed her eccentric style and made Lily No. 10 in its Best-dressed List of 2006.

Lily's music is celebrated for her skill in blending new and old, alternative and commercial, sweet and dark into something that sounds completely original but accessible. She has that same eye for fashion as she does for music.

She has a collection of over 300 new and vintage dresses. 'I'm just big into retail, generally. It's pretty shallow of me, but ever since I was younger, when I'd get my pocket money, I'd go shopping. I've always loved buying the new stuff that no one else has yet. I'd go to the soccer and wear dresses with really high heels. Then when I'd go out and all my friends were in dresses and heels, I'd wear a dress with trainers.'

Lily had become an overnight style icon, but she wasn't doing it for the glitz and glamour. She had an inherent hunger for design. 'Fashion design is something that I've always dreamed of doing. If I didn't work in music, I'd work in fashion in some way. But first and foremost, designers are the most important part of this industry. I really love the creative process. I don't want to be going to fashion parties and hanging out with models. I don't care for that.'

She would soon get a taste for design when Nike asked her to create her own trainers. For the girl who has more than 550 pairs of trainers at home – many of them Nike – she was understandably thrilled. 'I really like Nike trainers! I'm quite open about the fact that it's like a guilty pleasure for me, with the sweatshop aspect.'

Lily was soon being courted by the biggest fashion labels, and was among the stars in the crowd at March 2007 Paris Fashion Week. She was in the front row at the Yves Saint Laurent Show in the Pompidou Centre, mingling with the A-list, albeit uncomfortably so. 'It was funny seeing Victoria Beckham and Katie Holmes and Kanye West all sitting round me, because I still sort of see myself as this kind of naff person no one like them would want to get involved with. A kind of Kerry Katona type.'

Lily would also show her face at the Stella McCartney Autumn 2007/Winter 2008 collection at the Palais de Chaillot beneath the Eiffel Tower, alongside Barbara Bach and Olivia Harrison, the wives of former Beatles Ringo Starr and George Harrison.

Everywhere she went, photographers chased her down the street, desperate to get a look at this generation's new style icon. She was now friends with the fashion industry and loving it. 'They made such a fuss over me. I get bags of stuff – I have to keep throwing it away and giving it to charity shops. Chanel are really great to me and Prada gave me a load of stuff when I was in New York, which was fantastic. When I think back to where I was a year ago, it's all totally surreal.'

Indeed it was, but Lily was rightly seen as the new face of fashion and Lagerfeld in particular was taking keen notice of her. 'Chanel is probably my favourite label in the world. I've always known about Chanel, but I always thought of it as an old ladies' label. Then they invited me to the show in Paris, and it was amazing. Then I went to Madame Chanel's apartment, which had been untouched since she died. And just looking around and seeing where all of her inspiration came from – the quilting, the camellias – I just think it's really interesting to have a label that has so much history.'

Rumours soon circulated that Lily was in fact set to design for the luxury fashion label, and speculation intensified after she was seen wearing Chanel dresses at her live shows. It seemed it would only be a matter of time before it became official. True to form, though, she had her sights set somewhere else and announced to the world in February 2007 that she would indeed be adding 'fashion designer' to her bulging CV – but not for Chanel.

Instead, the singer signed a £250,000 deal with high-street chain New Look. She was to design six trademark frocks in a number of styles as well as jewellery and footwear for the Lily Loves range, to feature in 312 New Look stores in the UK, France, Dubai and Belgium. The look was unveiled in May 2007, and featured an ad campaign shot by fashion snapper Ellen von Unwerth. Renowned for its youthful images and bright colours, the photographer's style portrayed the Lily lifestyle perfectly.

Sarah Walter, head of fashion communication at the chain, which was founded in 1969, gushed about their new star designer: 'Lily is young, very talented, gorgeous, opinionated and feisty and we think a lot of our customers will identify with that.'
Lily says of the line, 'There's six dresses, all very different but all very me. They approached me last year and I did up some designs that they really liked.'

In a weird coincidence, Lily was paired with the girl she was compared to in her younger years, Drew Barrymore, who was also drafted in to be the face of a brand-new spring/summer clothing collection designed by Giles Deacon for New Look.

Lily would also find herself going head-to-head with two other celebrities who were turning their hands to fashion design: Madonna, who launched her M collection for New Look's high-street rivals H&M just months before; and Kate Moss, who had signed a deal with Topshop.

Madonna's spokesperson said the pop star 'has chosen the best pieces from her wardrobe and we have recreated them' and that the look 'reflects Madonna's fashion sensibilities, modern elegance and femininity'.

Supermodel Moss was recruited by Topshop's billionaire owner Sir Philip Green to create a 90-piece collection for the store. It was being touted at the start of 2007 as 'the most eagerly awaited clothing line ever'.

But Lily disagreed. She considered herself a positive role model and intended her collection to promote a healthy body image. She feared Topshop and Kate Moss were doing the opposite, and fumed, 'I like what New Look are doing and I like what they are about. They have responsible role models like me and Drew Barrymore and they're very conscious of having positive body images and promoting positive women. Unlike Kate Moss and that fucking billionaire who's thrown a load of money at her so we get to see what her wardrobe is like. It's madness.'

City analysts were impressed with the chains' celebrity tie-ins – considering them a good move. Rita Clifton, chairman of the brand consultancy Interbrand, said, 'The idea of using celebrities in some way is as old as marketing itself... What is interesting is the movement from endorsement (by celebrities) to active engagement.' She described the status of 'celebrity' as fragile but because high-street fashion is so fast-moving, if one goes into decline they can be replaced almost immediately.

However, as Peter Ruppert at Entertainment Media Research insisted, that was unlikely to be a problem for Lily, as her 'emotional attachment' rating was well above average for 13- to 19-year-old females and also above average in the 20- to 29-year-old demographic, making her an ideal partner for New Look. It also boded well for her music career. Those figures showed she had a big and strong fan base interested in absolutely everything she turned her hand to.

Lily took her new role seriously, and her blast at Kate Moss was not just a flippant comment taken out of context. Positive body image is a subject close to her heart and she has often spoken of her dismay at the image-obsessed culture we live in, where body weight is constantly held under scrutiny and dissected and pored over by 'experts'.

'I remember about five, ten years ago where it was, like, if the star has put on two stone, then it was on the front cover of magazines – because two stone is quite a lot of weight to put on. Now, it's like,

"Ooh, look, this star has a bit of fat." It's not fair. You will see a magazine with Jade Goody telling you how to get a swimsuit body in four weeks. And you know exactly what the fuck it will say – grilled chicken every night with vegetables for two weeks. And yeah, of course you're going to lose weight. That's obvious.

'Even I'm guilty of it. "Ooh, look, Jade Goody can tell me how to lose weight in two weeks. And I spend £3.50 on the stupid magazine. It's the fashion magazines I hate most. I'm now in a position where people send me free clothes and none of them fit me, and I'll tell you why – because they are samples, and samples are what the models they use get. And no one looks like models except for models. It's unhealthy and it's not a good look.

'I was talking to a friend of mine about this weight issue for women and he said, "Guys don't like skinny women." And I thought, What makes you think it's about men? It isn't actually. It's more about women. Anyway, because I'm a bit of a fuck-off person, I want to be a bit chubbier than most. If there's going to be little girls listening to Lily, I'd like them to think, She writes good songs and she's also not saying we have to be skinny.'

In a later rant, she said, 'I'd like to tell all those

fashion magazine editors out there to fuck right off, because I think we're all right as we are, ladies. When kids are looking through gossip magazines, and they see Posh Spice with these £800 bags, they don't know what to do. Then people go on things like *Pop Idol* and get rinsed by Simon Cowell. I did a lot of travelling when I was 17, 18, and I went to places like Cambodia and their quality of life is bad, but they keep smiling. The fact they don't have BMWs and McDonald's shoved in their faces is a good thing. That's what's wrong with youth culture today.'

Even fresh-faced Lily was the subject of unflattering commentary from celebrity fashion magazines. On her MySpace blog, she wrote, 'As usual I feature in the circle of shame section of *Heat* magazine this week, although this time not for walking to the shops without a couture dress, spray tan and piles of make up.

'Yes, a lovely paparazzi got down on the floor and took a picture directly up my nose. The caption reads something along the lines of "glow-in-the-dark bogeys". Now of course, like everybody else in the world, the inside of my nose consists of some moist matter that might shine when a huge fuck-off camera flash is pointed at it, the same exact way that my lip gloss and forehead do in the same picture. I wouldn't like to speculate what the magazine in question was trying to insinuate but they were wrong.'

Heat wasn't the only magazine unimpressed by Lily's growing fashion-icon status. Lily won the Worst Dressed award at the 2007 *NME* awards. But considering that she was living it up at Paris Fashion Week when the awards were announced, and that her highly public feud with the magazine was suspected to have played a part in the 'win', it was pretty much forgotten about instantly.

Feisty, talented and a huge
star, Lily Allen has had
hits around the world.
© WENN

Top: Lily has always got on with irreverent presenter and comedian, bad-boy Russell Brand, and guested on his E4 and MTV shows.

Below: Her appeal is very broad, and she is equally at home on Richard and Judy's sofa promoting the single 'Alfie', as she is talking to Jonathan Ross on his hit Friday night show or discussing her five favourite records of all time with Jayne Middlemiss on ITV1's *Orange Playlist* (*right*)   © *WENN*

Top left: When Lily accidentally parked her sporty Mini Cooper in a spot reserved for residents, she ended up with a fine. Despite her bad-girl image, this clearly left her distraught (*top right*).

Bottom: Lily's hymn to her home town, 'LDN', didn't mention the limos to exclusive restaurant Nobu or attending film premieres with brother Alfie (*bottom right*)!

© *WENN*

For millions of teenage fans, Lily is a style icon. Her distinctive look led fashion retailer New Look to recruit her as a designer for a range of dresses, shoes and accessories. (*right*) She has also been praised for speaking out about skinny models. © *WENN*

'If I didn't work in music, I'd work in fashion in some way.' Top left:
Performing in a customised dress. *Bottom left*: Hanging out with pal
Kelly Osbourne at London Fashion Week

At the 2006 V Festival, Lily stands out from the crowd. © WENN

Top left: Outside a London nightclub with model Agyness Deyn.

Above: Leaving the trainers at home for a more sophisticated look, Lily has a laugh filming the video for 'Littlest Things'.

Left: Lily with Ed Simons from the Chemical Brothers.

'I have worked hard but at the same time some of it is down to having the gift of the gab.' Lily goes from strength to strength. © *WENN*

CHAPTER NINETEEN
LILY'S LOVES

> 'I just want to be back in bed with my boyfriend having a hug.'

When 'Smile' was released in June, its sunny tone set the atmosphere perfectly for the hottest summer in Britain for years. The tune evoked memories of walks in the parks, ice cream and sunbathing. However, while Lily was promoting the song she had, for a long time, also been nursing a secret heartbreak. She had broken up with her long-term boyfriend Seb Chew.

Coupled with the stresses of promoting 'Smile', it was a traumatic split. She remarked at the time, 'I'm knackered. I'm also quite depressed because I've split up with my boyfriend. This should be the happiest time in my life but to be honest, I feel alone and lost and find myself crying uncontrollably.'

Only Lily could find herself in a situation where the biggest day of her life was overshadowed by another setback. It seemed every silver lining had a cloud. At the time she sighed, 'I know I should be sitting there going, "Yes! Fantastic! I'm No. 1." I should be enjoying life, but to be honest with you, I really don't feel like it. I just want to be back in bed with my boyfriend having a hug.'

Career-wise, the timing of the break-up was terrible, as everyone was chasing a piece of Lily. But the pop newcomer put on a brave face and behaved like a media veteran by committing to her promotional responsibilities dutifully.

Lily and Seb had met in 2005 while she was a regular at weekly club night YoYo at the Notting Hill Arts Club, which Seb ran with pal Leo Greenslade. After being introduced through friends, Lily and Seb, an A&R man who discovered the pop band Scissor Sisters, started dating.

Their relationship was happy and remarkably low-key and when they split it was heartbreaking for Lily. Lily found relationships tough, so to lose someone she had bonded so closely with was agonising.

Lily thought she was a good girlfriend, she was attentive, loved being affectionate and enjoys the thrill of just being alone with someone she loves while making scrambled eggs and toast, which she and Seb would eat in bed together. Describing her perfect date, she revealed, 'You know what, I'm not really one that likes to go out. I kind of like to just stay in and watch TV and talk and maybe eat pizza or something. Simple. And cheap. I'm a cheap date.' However, she admits, 'Boys make me mental. I'm really bad and attention-seeking and not a particularly nice person in relationships.'

It didn't help that while trying to recover from a second broken heart after her split with Seb, she was constantly being reminded about the man who broke it the first time.

After the success of 'Smile', which was written about Lester Lloyd, the press were determined to find out about the makings of the hit. Lily finally gave the *Sun* the story the media had all wanted. She opened up about her break with Lester.

'When I started writing music, "Smile" was the first thing I ever wrote. I always thought you should write about what you know, what's going on in your life, and this guy had taken up so much of my time and my emotions that the words just came pouring out. It was never going to be a sugar-sweet love song because by that time I was over him and felt a slight desire to get revenge through a song. So the lyrics are definitely bittersweet. Of course, I never thought the record would chart – I didn't even think I'd get a record contract.

'Then the record got to No. 1 and everyone asks if I feel it is a revenge story and I guess it is – but the truth is it's too painful for me to think of it in that way. It's a period of my life that I would rather not go back to. But anyway, things are now much happier for me. Discovering that I had a talent for making music really turned my life around.'

Lester recalled the first time he heard the record. He had finally got back from Thailand and went round to see Lily. She was a much stronger person than she was during their time together. Her spell at rehab and therapy had changed her for the better, restoring much-needed confidence, and she was focusing on writing songs.

'By the time I got home she was getting herself together again,' said Lester. 'I went round to her house to see the dog we had together. We'd spoken a few times and were friendly enough. She told me she had a new song she wanted to play me and put it on her car's CD player. It was "Smile". I listened to the lyrics and started grinning. I said: "This is about us, isn't it?" She said it was. The only line that didn't make any sense was "Doing the girl next door". I don't know why she's saying that. I've never cheated on Lily and never would. I know she's telling everyone that I slept with her best friend, but it's rubbish. I don't even know which friend she means.

'The rest was spot-on. Just like in the second verse, I knew she was "lost back then" but that with the help of her friends she found the light at the end of the tunnel. I know I messed up her "mental health" too, just like she sings, and I know I used to ring her with "a whine and a moan". Whenever it comes on the radio, my friends think it's hilarious. I'm still friends with lots of Lily's friends and they all know the history of the song. To me, and to them and my family, who also know and still like Lily, it's just Lily's song. Of course it's weird for the No. 1 song to be about me, but it is just a song.'

Lily found it hard talking about Lester – but it would get worse. After the success of 'Smile' he called her. While they talked Lily felt good about herself and she realised she really was finally over him. It was a comfortable talk until he dropped the bombshell – he had sold his story to the *Sunday Mirror*. She was devastated but showed remarkable composure when she heard the news. 'I couldn't really get angry with him because then he would have been really mean about me, so I just said, "OK."'

In the article Lester talked openly about the most intimate of details and recounted every drop of drama in their 18-month relationship, including how they got 'high every day smoking huge cannabis joints' and popped countless ecstasy pills at all-night parties. He then went on to boast about the time the couple had shared four pills of the drug and had passionate sex just yards away from thousands of club-goers. He said, 'We were both off our heads. The sex was out of this world. It went on for ages. We found a bit of soft ground to lie on and Lily slipped out of her jeans. She was wearing the cutest pair of knickers. She slipped out of those too and we began kissing. I'd never had sex outdoors before. It was a wild night and typical of Lily. She took the lead. She loved being on top. We made love for hours. Afterwards, we got dressed, went back to the rave and danced until the sun came up.'

When Lily finally got around to reading the article she was stunned that Lester was telling the world everything about their time together, and was embarrassed and hurt by the mistrust. 'I don't give a shit about him. He sold his story about me to the *Sunday Mirror* – like, sex and all, for £20,000. It really annoyed me, actually, because he sold his story for an hour and a half of talking. He got about as much as I signed a record deal for, and it took me three and a half years to make that album. It angered me so much. I put in all that work, and he broke my heart and fucked me over, and now he and his girlfriend are living in New York through me. The advance I got for my album had to last me over two years! He was my first love, which felt sacred. I wouldn't have been as upset if it was one of the others. I didn't love reading about it in the papers – my grandparents didn't either. Spineless bastard.'

But Lily was quick to claim she had already exacted her own revenge. 'I slept with all his friends, actually. The record could be a form of revenge if I cared what my ex-boyfriend thought, but I don't. But if I did want to upset him, I guess writing an album about him would be a good way.'

Lily found another form of revenge at the Secret Garden festival in July 2006. Both she and Lester were there, although they were at different ends of the spectrum. Lily was there as a pop star with thousands of fans going out of their way to see her perform, while Lester was with his girlfriend in a tent positioned directly opposite the main stage. Lily gleefully recalled the event, saying, 'He and his new girlfriend had no option but to watch me perform to a couple of thousand people singing "Smile" back to me. Oh, it's the little things, eh?'

And when people ask her what she thinks of him now, she says, 'If you Google Lester Lloyd, he sold his story to the papers so you can see exactly what he thought there.'

Lily was single, successful and cool, and happy to let her hair down, so surely it was only a matter of time before Cupid struck again. Not that she would go with just anyone. Once again, she breezed through the industry like a breath of fresh air when she claimed that, unlike other pop starlets who immediately latch on to the nearest available pop singer, she had her romantic sights set on more homely men. 'I like big chubby guys with glasses, bald head and back hair. There's no one in particular. I just like men rather than boys. Someone like David Beckham would be my idea of hell. I would sleep with him for a million quid. But I'd do just about anything for a million quid.'

Lily was enjoying being single and stated that she wanted 'to have a really exciting block of ten, fifteen years, then marry someone with enough money, get a house in the country and have lots of kids.'

She was soon finding herself linked with every celebrity bachelor going, as the press tried to play matchmaker for the broken-hearted pop star. It was rumoured that Lily was trying to romance her friend Nick Love but the director of *The Football Factory* was having none of it. Press reports suggested Lily was constantly sending him text messages. But Love laughed off the rumours, insisting he was closer to her mum Alison: 'She's a mate. I'm friends with her mum. I called her and she said, "Come on, man, I've got a No. 1 single. Of course people are going to make stuff up."'

Lily caused a stir when she did an interview in Australia with Andy Lee, of Fox FM's drive-time programme *Hamish & Andy*, in August. She quickly became quite enamoured with the man who had made the Top Fifty of *Cleo* magazine's annual hunt for Australia's most eligible bachelor.

When she played a gig at St Jerome's in Melbourne, Lily dedicated a song to Lee, before declaring she was in love with him. And on her MySpace blog she wrote about her tour of Australia, saying, 'I kissed the DJ after the show.' Lee insisted, however, that they were never an item. 'Lily has obviously gone back to England. I am not sure whether she flies into every city and dedicates a song to a radio host. It was very flattering, but I am not sure how seriously I can take that any more, considering she is on the other side of the world.'

She was also linked to the Klaxons' Jamie Reynolds. A source told the *Sun*: 'Lily and Jamie have become very close. He's a very funny man and she likes that. Lily's not lacking in the wit department either so it's a bit of a rally of observations and asides between them. It's early days yet but everyone reckons this could be the real thing for these two. All being well, they'll step out publicly at the Brits. After that they'll no doubt party hard at the *NME* Awards.'

Unfortunately for Jamie and the *Sun*'s prediction makers, Lily was not going to the Brits with Jamie, as in December she had announced she was back with Seb. Their romance was rekindled thanks to the single release of the poignant 'Littlest Things'. 'It got me my boyfriend back. We'd been broken up a couple of months when it came out and he must have heard it and realised how special I am. And he welcomed me back with open arms.'

She was overjoyed at getting Seb back, and she was determined to make it work the second time around, and actually welcomed the breaks they would have from each other while she travelled the world touring. 'It's kind of nice being away from each other because you don't have so much of the arguments and when you do see each other it's more special,' she revealed.

To celebrate getting back together, the pair flew to Jamaica for a romantic break to see in the New Year. For Lily, it was the perfect end to a crazy, party-filled year.

Friends of the pop star knew Seb was the one for her and were delighted when she told them the DJ was back in her life. Not that her assistant Emily's job was going to get any easier. Unsurprisingly, wannabe boyfriends constantly hounded Lily. The problem was, Lily couldn't spot the telltale signs and would happily talk to guys for ages not realising the feelings they had for her. Luckily, Emily would drag her away if she thought guys were getting too close. 'When you're in a relationship you kind of have that air about you. People kind of stay away. Actually, my assistant, Emily, travels everywhere with me and says I'm really, really bad at knowing when guys are coming on to me. She just drags me away from them and says, "He's not trying to be your friend!"'

Lily was in love and it made her legions of fans

happy. But they knew she would be fine anyway. Even if Lily is single, she's always got her trusted canine companion Maggie May.

CHAPTER TWENTY

PUPPY LOVE

'It feels like I've lost a child. I'm beside myself.'
JEREMY GOODMAN

Typically for Lily, just when it looked like everything was perfect, disaster struck. As she baked in the festive Caribbean heat with Seb, she received a phone call. Maggie May had been dognapped two days after Christmas.

Maggie's dog-walker Jeremy Goodman was preparing to take her to a pal of Lily's so she could stay there for a while when thieves raided his van outside his house in east London. Oddly, the thieves only targeted Maggie May, despite the presence of two other pedigree dogs in the van.

A tearful Lily was in shock when she came off the phone. Spending time with Maggie was her favourite thing in the whole world and she was constantly seen relaxing in Primrose Hill with the English bull terrier. Those walks would be a blessed relief from the stresses of the industry, and now it looked as if her beloved pet was gone for ever. For Lily, it was like losing a member of the family. Too upset for words, she immediately flew home in the hope she could find her precious pooch.

Meanwhile, her devastated dog-walker was scouring the neighbourhood to find Maggie. He said, 'I'm prepared to offer a reward. I just want her back. Distressed isn't even the word, it feels like I've lost a child. I'm beside myself. I've been everywhere to look for her, I've put up posters. All I've got to say to whoever's taken her is give her back. I've spoken to Lily and she's very upset. She's even cut short her holiday in Jamaica because she wants to come back and look for her.'

Lily frantically blogged her fans on MySpace to tell them about the situation and pleaded for anyone who had information to get in touch. 'I am beside myself with worry because someone has stolen my dog Maggie May this morning. I am in Jamaica, while I am here a friend has looked after Maggie. She was stolen out of his van outside his house and no one has seen her since. Not only am I devastated that my dog has been taken away, but I am also concerned for her wellbeing. She needs an operation on her stomach and is having medical treatment. There is a reward. Please anyone help. No one will be angry – my family and me just want Maggie home.'

Soon Lily joined Jeremy in the search for Maggie and, touchingly, fans of the singer were so moved by her MySpace plea that they helped with the search too. They exhausted themselves looking for Maggie but it seemed fruitless. Lily even called the company DogLost, which helps owners trace pets, but to no avail. It looked like Maggie had gone for good and Lily had finally given up hope of finding her.

Then she received a phone call. The caller claimed they had found a dog that looked like Maggie, and asked if she wanted her and would there be a reward.

Overjoyed, Lily met the caller in a quiet spot in Leytonstone, east London, and she was shocked by what she saw. It was Maggie all right but a much thinner one and, later inspection revealed, covered in fleas. It didn't matter to Lily and she threw her arms around the dog she thought she had lost. She quickly gave the group of people who 'found' Maggie an unspecified amount of money.

Lily suspected they were responsible for Maggie's disappearance, particularly because the group of young men and women offered to sell more puppies to her friends.

When she got back into her car with Maggie she pieced together what had happened. 'It made me realise that these people were obviously in the business of moving dogs. Now I feel guilty for having given them the money but I love my dog and had no choice. The fact that she was very thin made me think she was not fed and she was infested with fleas. The matter is now being handled by the police and the RSPCA [Royal Society for the Prevention of Cruelty to Animals].'

When news of the Lily Allen dognapping broke to the press it became clear that Lily wasn't the first to be duped by this scheme. Figures revealed that more than 2,000 pets are reported stolen in Britain each year, with some dognappers demanding over £2,000.

Lily quickly let her fans know of the situation: 'I have the best news ever. Maggie May is back at home safe and sound. She is riddled with fleas, a bit sad and very thin, but that's not the point. I can't tell you how overjoyed I am to have her back and how grateful I am to everyone who has sent kind words and helped to find her. I now know there is definitely some sense of community and goodwill left in this country, contrary to what some people might say. Anyway, it's late and I have only just got her back. Maggie's so tired now. But everyone wants to let her know how loved she is.'

She has had a long love affair with animals – and Maggie May had a special significance to her. When Lily and Lester were together, they weren't the only ones in the relationship. They had an adorable English bull terrier named Stella. When they split up, Lester's parents looked after the dog for a year. Despite the less-than-amicable split and the sour aftermath, Victoria and Julian are still very fond of Lily and would let her visit Stella whenever she liked. A family friend of the Lloyds told the Irish *News of the World*, 'She is really well liked by the family. No one has a bad word to say about her.'

Lily never took up the offer because of the distances involved, but when she played T In The Park in Scotland in June 2006 she decided to pay a quick visit to Ireland as Stella had had puppies and Lily was going to choose one to take home with her.

It was midnight before she rolled up to the Lloyds' house, a little bit drunk and with nine other drunken friends in tow. They loudly and merrily went to look at the puppies. Lester's parents were thrilled to see her and were happy that one of Stella's puppies was going home with what felt like family. Lily immediately picked the cutest one there – a little white bundle of joy. Her name would be Maggie May.

She fell in love with the precious puppy and excitedly logged on to her MySpace account to tell her fans about the new love in her life. 'She's called Maggie May and she's very bitey. I have scars on my hands where her sharp teeth break the skin.' Luckily, help was on hand in the guise of her brother Alfie, who was doing his best to toilet-train Maggie. 'On the plus side Alfie has managed to make her pee and poo on newspaper, which is great! I love her so much,' Lily enthused.

Now, half a year later, with a loving boyfriend, stable family and her beloved dog back, Lily's home life was as good as ever.

But drama and another big bombshell were never far away. Very soon her father's womanising past was to catch up with him in a shocking way.

CHAPTER TWENTY-ONE

FAMILY REUNION

'I'll be quite honest with you – nobody knows how many kids I've got, there's a rumour it's seven.'
KEITH ALLEN, THE OBSERVER, 2000

With Lily's new-found success and her father's fondness for being Jack the Lad, it was inevitable the two would eventually and publicly clash – particularly over the subject of Keith's other children.

Lily was on the bill at the UK festival the Big Chill in August 2006 and was just about to perform when her father came over with his newest family addition, Teddie, from his relationship with his girlfriend, actress Tamzin Malleson. Despite 20,000 fans screaming her name, Lily stayed to play with little baby Teddie, just a month old – and was beaming about the amount of fun that was to be had being the older sister to this beautiful baby girl.

The show itself was a massive success. Whether it was playing with Teddie or the pint of Magners that she had downed before she went on stage or the deafening screams of applause, she tackled the set with a commanding confidence. Alfie, determined not to be overshadowed by his two siblings, showed what he could offer by having a little dance on stage when his song – 'Alfie' – came on.

Lily said at the time, 'My Glastonbury [even though it wasn't Glastonbury] dream came true, people did jump up and down and we [the band] had a great time. My dad came back to see me after and he was *sooo* proud he was almost crying.'

Keith was indeed so proud of his family. He has often talked in interviews in the past about his love for Alfie and Lily, but he did have other children, and it's clear they haven't all enjoyed the benefits of his fathering skills.

Lily's half-brother Kevin Marshall was serving six months in prison for stealing cars when he received word he had a visitor. His cell door was opened and he was told, 'Your sister is here.' He hadn't seen her for years, but true enough it was Lily. She was 16 then and she was clutching a package for him, containing a tracksuit and trainers.

It was an emotional reunion, and one that both were desperate for. At that stage in Lily's life she was very much in a transitional period after the drama of her Ibiza holiday and Kevin was desperate for some family comfort. The pair had always got on. As a child growing up, Kevin would travel from his west London council estate home to his father's luxury house in north London to play with Lily. But as the years went on they drifted apart and Kevin was eventually sent to Feltham Young Offenders Institute in 2002. That was when Lily met him: 'I could tell she was upset to see me in a cell, but when she walked in I was so happy. She brought me a tracksuit and trainers. She said she wanted us to be more of a family when I got out and that she didn't want to see me in places like this again.'

Kevin was born after his father had a fling in 1982 with a shop assistant called Sandra Marshall. He had a rocky relationship with his father but insists he respects Keith for saying he felt unable to love him after his birth.

It didn't matter to Kevin as he struck up a friendship with Lily once he was released, for the first time since they were little children. One day when they were hanging out she produced a CD of a couple of her songs. One of them was 'Smile', and Kevin instantly knew that it was a No. 1 hit. He would be two years early with his prediction. The other song took his breath away as soon as he heard it, he was so moved. The song was called 'Nasty Business' and it told the story of how Kevin, like his dad, spent time behind bars. It has never been released.

Despite the close bond they were forming, Lily's pleas for him to turn his back on a life of crime went unheeded and he later served six months in Wandsworth for dealing marijuana.

As Lily has become more and more famous, Kevin hardly ever sees his favourite stepsister. 'It's hard to keep in touch with Lily now she's famous. We were close but I can't even speak to her without going through her people now. I sometimes hope that she'll just give me a call.'

Another of Keith Allen's kids spoke out against her father to the *News of the World* in March 2007. Grace Peters was born in 1985 to mum Linda Peters. She has never had a strong relationship with Keith, admitting that she didn't meet her father until she was 15, and then had to explain who she was. They met at Keith's favourite watering hole, the Groucho Club. They haven't seen each other for the past two and a half years.

'He was stunned that I had a job,' said Grace. 'He couldn't understand me. I'm normal. There's not much more to our relationship than meeting for a chat and a drink every few years. I didn't want or need anything from him. I have a good life. I haven't seen Keith for two and half years. He'd have to admit he's not a good advert for a parent. He'd only know who I was if he saw me down the street because I'm a spit of Lily – I've never gone looking for Daddy – Mum is all I've ever needed.'

Linda Peters once claimed that when she was pregnant, Keith asked if it was his. 'No,' she replied, 'it's mine.' But Keith denied her side of the story: 'That's all rubbish. Well, it's her side of it.'

Another mother of one of Keith's kids accused him of ignoring his own daughter Galoushka. He had a two-year on-off relationship with jazz singer Anjel Tabatha (also known as Anje Talbott) and they split for good in 1991. The parting was not amicable. Galoushka (Gala for short) was born in 1990, but it was only a year later that Keith admitted he was the father after a magistrate ordered a DNA test.

In 1994 he was ordered to pay for his daughter's

upkeep. Anjel said, 'Since day one I have had to fight tooth and nail to make him face up to his responsibilities.

'Keith has forced me to confront him in court ever since Gala was born. First he denied the baby was his. Then I had to fight for maintenance.

'By the time I was about to give birth he had already had an affair with Nira Park. And he was with Alison in the Caribbean when I was giving birth three days before Christmas. When he came back he phoned and asked: "What did Father Christmas give you?" That's how seriously he took it.'

In 1997 Keith won an injunction against Anjel for harassment after she persistently telephoned and visited his home.

In 2000, when Gala was ten, her mother revealed a telling moment in an interview: 'The other day I heard her crying on the phone because he said she would have to forget him for a few more years.

'Then he apparently said: "Don't cry. You're not missing anything. We don't even really know each other. I'll see you when you're 16," and put the phone down. It's not very amusing to be around someone so high on his own personality. He's completely egotistical and what might seem funny in a television script can be cruel in real life. He has great highs and terrible lows. We've had some spectacular rows and I'd never want to go through that again. These days I loathe him so much I turn the television off when I see him.'

However, Keith sees it differently, insisting kids don't inherently need a father figure. 'I think it's an insult, actually, to women, to single women. I think kids are nurtured by an extended family, anyway: your friends, your peer group at school, whatever. And it isn't necessarily about family. I've always questioned that. Always. And it's not to say that blood-is-thicker-than-water doesn't exist. It palpably does. But it's kind of interesting how people embrace it.'

In an interview in 2000, Keith looked back at his parenting skills with Lily and Alfie with a twinge of regret. But he dismissed claims he has been an errant father, ticking off his kids' names with his fingers, 'One child, the mother wanted because she needed a companion for her son, and one's a complete idiot – I won't mention her name – who is bringing up her daughter with a view to hating me, which is fine for me, but it's awful for the child. But she'll have a choice when she's older. I've always maintained, if the children want me, I'll be there. Not that the son I recently met had much choice – I had to go and get him out of prison.'

It must have been hard for Lily to be around this sort of family drama, especially when played out in the media throughout her life. She has never denied her dad's faults but she has not been slow to defend him either. She recognises there are two sides to every story, but all she's ever wanted was for her entire family to be friends with each other. Kevin, Grace and Gala would be mentioned in the sleeve notes for Lily's debut album *Alright, Still*: 'I wish I saw more of you.'

But, as Grace puts it, 'I can't see Keith having a big reunion for us all.'

CHAPTER TWENTY-TWO

LILY DEALS WITH FAME

'I guess it's something that I fantasised about, but it's turning out to be very different to what I imagined.'

By the end of 2006 Lily had laid claim to being the pop sensation of the year. End-of-year polls in magazines and newspapers went out of their way to namecheck Lily – whether it was for her music, her look or her outspoken qualities. What no one could argue about was that she had made her mark in a spectacularly short time. She even had time to come fourth in girl magazine *Sugar*'s poll for most inspirational celebrity of 2006 behind Hilary Duff, Christina Aguilera and winner Kylie Minogue. Lily was the highest-placed British girl on the list.

It's not hard to see why her legion of fans empathised with her so much. Here was a fully-fledged pop star who refused to shield her inner thoughts. Lily was one of them – streetwise, emotional, tough, sensitive and bemused by the alien world that fame can offer, and she was quick to let her fans know about it. She remembered one occasion, shortly after 'Smile' got to No. 1, when she attended the same party as a group of D-list celebrities and was summoned over to them. As you can imagine, this did not go down too well with Lily. She recalled, 'There's a world of celebrities in the UK and nothing makes you more sick than when you walk into a room of celebrities and they give you this celebrity nod and kind of invite you into their group. No, thank you. I don't really want to be in your weird group. I don't care if any of those people are offended.'

And Lily showed another string to her bow. Appearing on the hit comedy panel show *Never Mind the Buzzcocks* on 30 November 2006, she easily stood toe to toe with heavyweight comedians Phil Jupitus and Bill Bailey and traded quips and banter with ease. When they were shown an old early 1990s music video clip of Catherine Zeta-Jones they were asked why she was in what looked to be an antique shop. Lily chimed in with, 'To buy Michael Douglas.' The panel and the audience loved her.

But Lily was finding fame to be more of a burden than she realised. She often claims in her blogs that she just wants to lie in her bed and cuddle up to her boyfriend and hang out with friends. The constant touring, the interviews and the attention leave her feeling stifled.

When she does manage to secure some time to herself she mainly stays in with her friends, waiting for them to come round with a few bottles of wine. She remains cooped up in her house, while making sure her curtains are closed to keep the paparazzi from seeing her. 'They're outside my house all the time and I have to keep my curtains drawn because my room looks out on to the street – it's annoying.'

When Lily first started blogging she would talk about her ideal day – 'today however I had a lazy day, got up, strolled down to the shops bought a croissant from Sainsbury's and a coffee from Nero's and sat on the doorstep reading the newspaper while smoking fags. HEAVEN. Then I did a few phone interviews and went for a walk in the sun. Now I'm in bed listening to old 7"s and writing blogs.'

It seemed back then that Lily was getting the best of both worlds; she could remain anonymous while getting the attention she craved as soon as she clicked 'send' on her blog page.

In a bid to regain some privacy, Lily confesses she buys pay-as-you-go mobile phones as she loves the idea of having secret numbers that nobody knows. Even her management sometimes can't get hold of her, much to Lily's amusement.

Because of her father's notoriety Lily has seen first-hand how the paparazzi work – and will more often than not play them at their own game. She hates the idea of other people making money out of her and it's not like she needs the exposure – her fans see pictures and videos of Lily all the time through her home-made photos and footage she posts on her blog. They are intimate and fun and show a relaxed side to her that sometimes the casual fans don't see. Whether it's larking around in a dinosaur outfit, stealing her guitarist's clothes while he is out swimming or dancing backstage to Kasabian, she constantly allows her fans privileged access to her life.

Paparazzi assigned to snap Lily admit she is a tough girl to handle. She is well versed in the workings of the media and knows how to play it. If they are seeking a funny picture of her, she knows to stand still and make it as boring as possible. When being followed in her car, she will wait at the green light for as long as she can, before speeding off just before the light turns red, leaving photographers unable to catch her.

One photographer once made the mistake of telling her how much money a good picture of her can command. Predictably, Lily made it her mission to stop him capturing her on film.

These are playful gestures that are commonplace in the cat-and-mouse world of the paparazzi, but Lily does have a temper, and when she snaps, they are often on the receiving end.

After her gig at London's Carling Apollo on 14 March 2007, the 'Smile' singer whacked one photographer and then attempted to wrestle a camera from another one – as they attempted to snap her leaving the venue. After the Brit Awards she lashed out at photographers with her stilettos.

Also in 2007 she snapped at a photographer who had been camped outside her house, hoping to get a picture of her. The paparazzo says, 'She got out of her car and started to walk towards me smiling, which I thought was a bit odd. Just as I was about to take pictures I noticed a bottle of Fanta or something in her hand which had previously been covered up with jacket. She threw all the contents over me. I was absolutely soaked. The next thing I knew her brother Alfie appeared telling me to leave his sister alone and Lily was screaming at me that she would get me hurt.'

Lily was, as always, looking for something to rebel against and react to. While growing up she had school to fight, but now she had nothing. She had her dream-of-a-lifetime job. She was travelling the world, meeting new people, receiving the acclaim she had always wanted and getting the platform to stretch as an artist. But it was starting to get to her – it wasn't as much fun any more.

It certainly didn't help that her family were making the headlines again. In February 2007, while Lily was in Paris attending a fashion shoot with Stella McCartney, it was reported that her mother Alison suffered a minor head wound after an alleged attack by her son Alfie at their north London home. Police questioned Alfie. One source told the *Sun*, 'It was a family argument that got out of hand. There was some argy-bargy which led to Alison calling the police. But I think she now wishes she hadn't dialled 999.'

A neighbour also told the paper, 'Two police cars converged on the house with blue lights flashing. It was very dramatic.'

Lily herself said, 'I love my family and I wish I had been there to help calm this situation down. I have spoken to my mum and Alfie and everything is fine now.'

She was working harder than she ever had in her life before and, with the prospect of trying to break America looming, it was clear she needed a release – something to rant at and to take her mind off the pressures of the job. She was to get one, and it wouldn't be the press but a fellow pop star.

CHAPTER TWENTY-THREE

GOING AWAY EMPTY-HANDED

> 'I already know I won't win any awards.
> I bet I'll get nothing.'

Arguably the two biggest British music awards ceremonies are the Nationwide Mercury Prize and the Brit Awards. They are remarkably different shows, apart from one factor – there would be someone heavily tipped as a winner for both who would end up walking away empty-handed twice.

The Nationwide Mercury Prize was established in 1992 by the BPI (British Phonographic Industry) and BARD (British Association of Record Dealers), and its main aim was to recognise and celebrate alternative music. Some saw it as the ideal alternative to the self-congratulatory, back-slapping awards shows. There was only one winner, with the decision made by the Mercury Prize judges, who were a group of powerful people within the industry.

Some critics have accused the show of giving the prize to underground acts ahead of established mainstream acts in a deliberate attempt to gain more publicity.

On 18 July the shortlist for the 2006 Mercury Prize was announced. Lily's record label was convinced she would get nominated as she ticked all the boxes. Her album was a chart success and her music was an amalgamation of styles from underground sensibilities to mainstream hands-in-the-air anthems. She was exactly the act the ceremony needed. They sat waiting for Lily's name to be called out among the dozen shortlisted acts. Nothing could go wrong – could it?

Arctic Monkeys – *Whatever People Say I Am, That's What I'm Not*
They were a popular choice, and would be Lily Allen's biggest challenge of the night. They not only used MySpace (or at least their fans did) to their advantage before Lily did, but their album was also the fastest-selling debut in UK chart history.

Muse – *Black Holes and Revelations*
The supersonic glam rock band's fourth album was their biggest-selling and best, with the Mercury judges calling it 'bold, brave and bright'. They had already angered Lily once before by 'stealing' the *NME* cover from her – surely they wouldn't steal the scene again, would they?

Isobel Campbell and Mark Lanegan – *Ballad of the Broken Seas*
Former cellist for indie band Belle and Sebastian, Campbell teamed up with the ex-lead singer of American rock band Screaming Trees for an album that was described as 'eerie and sensual, sweet and sinister, evocative and remarkable'.

Zoe Rahman – *Melting Pot*
The jazz artist's 2001 debut album, *The Cynic*, with drummer Winston Clifford and bassist Jeremy Brown, was shortlisted for the BBC Radio 3 jazz album of the year review in 2001.

Editors – *The Back Room*
Fronted by Tom Smith – whose girlfriend is Radio 1 DJ Edith Bowman – the band's gloomy, 1980s-style rock met with the approval of the judges, who called

the album 'edgy, forceful and compelling – a hugely impressive debut'.

Lou Rhodes – *Beloved One*
This female singer-songwriter was one half of Lamb, best known for its track 'Gorecki'.

Lily's people looked on knowingly. So far there were no big surprises. Big-name bands, at least one jazz act and a smattering of low-key groups. Lily was sure to be called out soon.

Guillemots – *Through the Windowpane*
The rock group defined boundaries, sitting comfortably in genres as far-ranging as pop, jazz and rock. The judges praised the band, saying they didn't think 'there's a greater art than writing a three-minute pop song'.

It was at this point that Lily's people thought they could have a problem. Guillemots were the exact act the show needed – a fresh-faced, mainstream band with alternative sensibilities. The only problem was, that slot was meant to be filled by Lily.

Scritti Politti – *White Bread, Black Beer*
Formed in the 1970s, this arty pop band had come up with its first album since 1999.

Richard Hawley – *Coles Corner*
The former Longpigs guitarist had played with the likes of All Saints and Robbie Williams. *Coles Corner* was 'a wonderfully unapologetic romantic' album, according to the judges.

That meant there were just three albums left.

Sway – *This Is My Demo*
The UK rapper had already pulled one shock by beating US superstars The Game and 50 Cent to win Best Hip Hop Artist at the 2006 Mobo's. Could he do it again?

Hot Chip – *The Warning*
Schoolfriends Joe Goddard and Alexis Taylor teamed up to make an electronic masterpiece, with the judges calling it an 'irresistible DIY electro pop – brilliantly realised.'

Now there was only one name left. There was still a barrage of big-name acts that had broken through, including the Kooks, Corinne Bailey Ray and the Zutons, that hadn't been called. Lily's people feared the worst. Then the last name was called out…

Thom Yorke – *The Eraser*
The frontman of the popular band Radiohead had filled the last nomination. Lily Allen had missed out. The judges hailed *The Eraser* as 'a compelling new setting for Thom Yorke's voice and lyrical vision'.

The next morning the shortlist divided opinion but the talking point throughout was the Lily-sized absence of a prize for original artistry, collaboration and genuine musical presence. The *Sun* called Lily's omission a shock, while the *Daily Telegraph* slammed the prize as 'irrelevant'. EMI Records' managing director Terry Felgate, however, looked at the bright side: 'There are a lot of records in this year's shortlist that can really benefit. It's a shame that Corinne and Lily weren't in there, but I do think it would be nice if the winner was an artist that was able to make a substantial jump.'

When told she failed to make the shortlist, Lily was as sharp-tongued as ever: 'It's nice to be nominated, but where are the past winners now?' she jibed.

The *Guardian* ran a story on one of the judges

who claimed Lily was 'the subject of intense debate', and that some of the jury thought 'she doesn't really mean it, and isn't very committed as a performer'. It was a pretty absurd assessment, and Lily wasn't slow to respond.

'I think that's a pretty stupid comment assuming the Mercury Music Prize is not about live performances. I worked really, really hard on this album. The prize is so treasured in this country, I'd be lying if I said I wasn't disappointed that I didn't get a nomination, because I felt like I made some really alternative pop music that deserves some recognition. There have been artists nominated for that award that I don't think have been as honest as I have, and haven't even written most of their records. But I suppose the prize is put there to help people, and I've sold a lot of albums already, so I'm not too mad about it. I'm definitely not going to stay up worrying about the Mercuries. And also there's always the Grammies!'

It was a setback for Lily's musical career, with the prize eventually going to her MySpace rivals Arctic Monkeys. But she wouldn't have to mope for much longer. A bigger awards ceremony was looming ever closer.

On 16 January the nominees for the 2007 Brit

Awards were announced, and it was much better news for Lily. In fact, it was great news. She was shortlisted for four prizes, including Best British Female Solo Artist, Best British Album, British Breakthrough Act and British single for 'Smile' – which would be decided by the public.

Rock band Muse had three nominations, for Best British Group, British Album and British Live Act. Dance stars Gnarls Barkley scored three nominations for Best International Group, Album and Breakthrough Act. Corinne Bailey Rae, James Morrison and Snow Patrol were each shortlisted three times, including a place on the Best British Single list.

So with four nominations Lily led the field for the ceremony on 14 February. It looked set to be a celebratory night for her. Former Pulp frontman Jarvis Cocker, who was nominated for Best British Male, heaped praise on Lily: 'I can tell her music is a good reflection of what she is, she hasn't been groomed for stardom.'

It was also a good night for the internet in general. The dominance of nominations for Lily Allen and Gnarls Barkley, who was the first act to get to No. 1 on downloads alone, proved the web was playing a huge part in the music industry.

For Best Female Solo Artist Lily was competing against Amy Winehouse, Corinne Bailey Rae, Jamelia and Nerina Pallot.

For Best British Album, the nominees were Arctic Monkeys *(Whatever People Say I Am That's What I'm Not)*, Amy Winehouse *(Back to Black)*, Lily Allen *(Alright Still)*, Muse *(Black Holes and Revelations)* and Snow Patrol *(Eyes Open)*.

For Best British Breakthrough Act, which was chosen by BBC Radio 1 listeners, she was up against the Fratellis, Corinne Bailey Rae, James Morrison and the Kooks. She was also up for Best British Single, but was weeded out of the final shortlist just before the show started.

The other nominations were: for Best British Male Solo: Jarvis Cocker, Lemar, James Morrison, Paolo Nutini and Thom Yorke. For Best British Group: Kasabian, Muse, Razorlight, Snow Patrol and Arctic Monkeys. For Best International Breakthrough Act: Gnarls Barkley, Orson, the Raconteurs, Ray Lamontagne and Wolfmother. For Best British Live Act: Muse, George Michael, Guillemots, Kasabian and Robbie Williams.

The final shortlist for Best British Single was: Take That ('Patience'), The Feeling ('Fill My Little World'), Razorlight ('America'), Snow Patrol ('Chasing Cars') and Will Young ('All Time Love'). For Best International Male Solo Artist the contenders were: Beck, Bob Dylan, Damien Rice, Justin Timberlake and Jack Johnson. Best International Female Solo Artist nominations were: Nelly Furtado, Beyonce, Cat Power, Christina Aguilera and Pink. For Best International Group: the Flaming Lips, Gnarls Barkley, the Red Hot Chili Peppers and the Scissor Sisters. Contenders for Best International Album were: Bob Dylan *(Modern Times)*, The Killers *(Sam's Town)*, Gnarls Barkley *(St Elsewhere)*, Justin Timberlake *(FutureSex/LoveSounds)* and the Scissor Sisters *(Ta-Dah)*. Finally, Oasis were nominated for Outstanding Contribution To Music.

It was a strong line-up. For British home-grown music, 2006 had proved to be an excellent year. This was a music climate in which manufactured pop was dying out and being replaced by true talent in guitar music, folk, R&B, soul, acoustic ballads and dance. It was a good time to be part of the industry.

The *Sun*'s Victoria Newton bumped into Lily's dad at the Groucho Club when the nominations were announced. Hearing about the nominations Keith drunkenly asked, 'What about mine for best dad?'

Lily was pensive. She might have put on a brave face and uttered a withering put-down after failing to get nominated for the Mercury Prize, but in truth it had hurt her. When making *Alright, Still* she would have presumed that if it had a fair chance of winning anything it would have been that. But it was an embarrassing shun and even the Brit Awards nominations didn't fill her with glee. Believing herself not to be good enough she glumly declared she didn't expect to take home anything. On one hand you could understand that she was a young girl who had already been left red-faced once and was simply lowering her expectations, but on the other it was a rather surprising defeatist attitude from someone leading in the nominations.

As she looked through the nominations again for Best Female, Lily genuinely believed she didn't stand a chance. If she was going to lose, she figured that it might as well be to someone she liked. So she quickly jumped in to pour scorn over Corrine Bailey Rae, calling her 'boring'. Ironically, it was Amy Winehouse she hoped would come out as a winner. With hindsight, maybe Lily should have been careful what she wished for.

Despite Lily's best effort, Corinne Bailey Rice would not be drawn into a slagging match. The 28-year-old songwriter, whose eponymous hit R&B debut album was released in February 2006, admirably declared, 'I've heard Lily say that [I am boring] before. I guess I'm not really her thing. I'm really excited about playing at the Brits but I wouldn't put any money on me to win anything. My album's been out for nearly a year. And Lily and Amy are really strong contenders for the Female Solo Artist.'

Lily wasn't convinced, and was adamant she would be going home a loser. 'There's the split vote thing going on when you are nominated in all those categories, but I think Amy Winehouse will win the Best Female award and I don't think I will win anything.'

She also didn't give herself a chance in the Best Breakthrough act category, which is decided by the public. She couldn't see past her old schoolmate Luke Pritchard's band the Kooks, because of the huge support from young girls who phone vote lines. She said, 'I think they'll walk it. When I heard about the nominations I felt like it was a bit of a burden. I hate being in competitions 'cos I never win. I was disappointed that I didn't get my Mercury nomination last year. When you do get nominated it's really nice, but at the same time I'm going to have to put on my "Oh, I'm really happy Corinne won" face, I know I am.'

It was a weird time for Lily, as this should have

been the moment she showed the industry she had made it, but she constantly downplayed her chances to the point where she said she might not even attend the event.

Luckily, Keith stepped in to save the day. Her father knew first-hand the fickle nature of the business and was determined that his daughter make the most out of this opportunity as he knew she would only be full of regrets otherwise. Lily recalled, 'My dad says part of being a pop star is walking down the red carpet wearing a nice dress and having your photo taken and he's right. I might not get the chance again.'

Aside from the Brit Awards, Lily was riding high. *Alright, Still* had sold half a million copies in Britain, and her attempt to do what no British act had achieved in years and break America was coming along nicely. A recent showcase in Los Angeles the previous October has managed to attract an A-list crowd including Gwen Stefani and Orlando Bloom.

But the Brits shadow loomed large and Lily wasn't allowed to forget that. She had already been told on the day that she hadn't made the final Best Single shortlist. Amy Winehouse missed out on Lily's omission from Best Single, which was voted by the public, as she was busy trying to text in for Lily!

On 14 February at London's Earls Court, Valentine's Day was forgotten about as the Brit Awards attempted to get underway. Lily did turn up, despite fears that the pop start might stay away after downplaying her chances for so long. Even the tabloids began to wonder if she was right, the *Sun*'s Victoria Newton boldly predicting that she would go away empty-handed.

Lily came bounding down the red carpet, however, looking stunning in a shimmering green dress and a yellow ribbon bunch nestling in her hair. She came with her dad and both milked the attention. On arrival she told MTV News: 'I already know I won't win any awards. I bet I'll get nothing. The judging committee are all industry insiders. They're mostly from Universal Records and I'm on EMI. I think you'll find 70 per cent of the artists here tonight are on Universal. I'll leave you with that.'

And then they went inside, and the ceremony for the biggest British music festival of the year started. The Brit Awards first began in 1971 under the title the British Phonographic Industry Awards. In 1989 it was renamed the Brit Awards. The 2007 show was to be the first one recorded live since the disastrous 1989 ceremony hosted by Samantha Fox and Mick Fleetwood. Live shows were axed after the pair read out names at the wrong time, forgot their cues and fluffed lines, creating classic car-crash television.

Although shows were pre-recorded following that debacle, there have been enough controversial moments in the show's years to keep us watching, including Jarvis Cocker's impromptu stage protest at Michael Jackson and John Prescott being soaked by a bucket of water thrown by the band Chumbawamba.

The event was themed around love and hate, with Oasis performing on the 'hate' stage and Take That appearing on the 'love' stage.

There would be little controversy during the actual show itself, although presenter Russell Brand managed to upset some viewers with several misguided quips about friendly-fire killings, sexual innuendo, Robbie Williams's stint in rehab and Amy Winehouse's battle with booze, with ITV receiving 300 complaints.

The real talking point was the awards themselves. Lily was right all along, and had every reason to be downbeat. She lost out on every nomination. The Best Female Solo Artist Award was snapped up by Amy Winehouse; Best British Album went to Arctic Monkeys; while the Fratellis scooped the Best Breakthrough Act.

Other winners of the night were: Best British Male Solo Artist: James Morrison; Best British Group – Arctic Monkeys; Best British Single – Take That ('Patience'); Best British Live Act – Muse; Best International Male Solo Artist – Justin Timberlake; Best International Female Solo Artist – Nelly Furtado; Best International Group – the Killers; Best International Album – the Killers *(Sam's Town)*; Best International Breakthrough Act – Orson; and Outstanding Contribution to Music – Oasis.

For Lily, it was a remarkable snub. For what looked like the perfect opportunity to toast a triumphant year, it had left a remarkably flat taste in the mouth. Deflated, she went to the Oasis after-show party to drown her sorrows.

Lily wasn't to know it, but things would get much worse for her. As well as leaving the awards ceremony empty-handed, she had also lost a good friend.

CHAPTER TWENTY-FOUR

FIGHTING TALK

'I'm a bitch. I'm like a gay man in a woman's body.'

When beaten to the Best Female award by Amy Winehouse, Best Album by Arctic Monkeys and Best Breakthrough Act by the Fratellis, what is a girl to do? Well, party, obviously. Lily was all dressed up with nowhere to go until Liam Gallagher grabbed her and took her to his band's after-party. The British hellraisers, celebrating their Outstanding Contribution trophy, took over the members' lounge at the Cuckoo Club – and promptly drank so much alcohol that extra ice had to be ordered in.

Lily may have been on a downer after her shock

loss but there was some small comfort in the fact she had been invited to this very exclusive party – especially because a few celebrities had been left red-faced after being refused entry. The reason? Noel Gallagher was personally vetting each guest, and was happy to reject ones he didn't think were good enough. He said, 'We're throwing our own party so we can snub people and not let them in.' Among those excluded were Brit winner James Morrison, Badly Drawn Boy, Madness's Suggs, Alex Zane, Sadie Frost and Jamie Cullum.

As the Oasis frontman and his fiancee Nicole Appleton left the club, chaos erupted outside as Allen waved her Christian Louboutin stiletto at a crowd of photographers, and Liam scrawled in marker pen on a paparazzo's camera lens. One onlooker said, 'The police had to be called because cars were getting scratched, people were getting squashed. Liam was just being his usual cocky self, which riled some fans who'd been waiting for autographs and they started chanting, "Who are you?" And Lily seemed to have the Liam snarl down to a tee.'

'I had a great time at the Oasis party. Liam and Nicole offered me a lift back to my hotel. There were so many photographers outside the party and it was hard to find my own car,' recalled Lily.

Post-Brits, the press had a field day, and immediately there was an autopsy on the event, with people dying to know why Lily had lost out on all her nominations. Was Lily right? Was there a giant conspiracy? Of the thirteen top awards, eight were given to Universal Group artists.

Despite the saying that no one remembers second place, it seems that was all anyone wanted to talk about. Lily was *the* talking point in the media.

A journalist reported that she said, 'I had a real slagging match with Amy Winehouse. It was terrible.' Lily has since protested that no such argument happened: 'The story about me being in tears either because I didn't win a Brit or had a fight with Amy is complete rubbish. She and I are friends and we were hanging out at the Brits and at the Oasis party afterwards. I was talking to her and Mark Ronson for ages. Mark is a mutual friend who produced Amy's album and mine.

'I always said that I wasn't expecting to win, and that if I wasn't going to win then I hoped Amy did. I'm very pleased for her. The pictures of me crying in the papers were taken when I was saying goodbye to my boyfriend who I haven't seen much of recently. I've been working really hard and travelling a lot and I only got to see him at the Brits so the tears were just because I was leaving to get on yet another plane.'

However, it soon became clear that something did indeed happen between Lily and Amy and their friendship would never be the same.

Amy Winehouse was born in north London in 1983. When she was ten she formed an amateur rap group called Sweet 'n' Sour with childhood best friend Juliette Ashby – which Amy later dubbed 'the little white Jewish Salt 'n' Pepa'.

The pair remained friends throughout school and Amy got her first taste of showbiz, working with Juliette at entertainment news agency World Entertainment News Network. She was there for several years, and even found herself writing news stories about stars and musicians who would soon become her fellow artists and performers.

Amy was always destined to be a singer and had been performing professionally since she was 16. She was quickly snapped up by Spice Girl creator Simon Fuller's 19 Management, who in turn helped her land a record deal with Island Records. As Island and 19 began grooming Amy for greatness she had to leave journalism behind – but it wasn't long before she was making headlines herself, when her debut album, *Frank*, smashed on to the scene in 2003.

Her heavily jazz-influenced sound was like a breath of fresh air for the British music scene and she very quickly picked up radio airplay, which in turn helped her album make its way up the charts and go platinum. It impressed the critics too, earning her two Brit Award nominations, a Mercury Prize nomination and an Ivor Novello songwriting award for 'Stronger Than Me'.

Amy disappeared from the music radar after *Frank* was released, only making the headlines for rumours about her love life, weight loss and alcohol intake. But in October 2006 she burst back with the release of her second album, *Back to Black*. She ditched the jazz sound of *Frank*, taking inspiration for the new disc – which was produced by Mark Ronson – from 'the girl groups of the 1950s and 60s'.

If her first album forced listeners to sit up and listen, *Back to Black* knocked them off their feet. And its ballsy and original sound earned it commercial and critical acclaim. The single 'Rehab' – about Amy's refusal to seek help for her excessive alcohol consumption – earned her her first Top Ten single in the UK charts. The album shot to No. 1 and has gone double platinum, selling more than 750,000 copies – more than three times what her first album managed in the same time. The critics loved it as well, with the album helping her pip Lily Allen to the Best Female Solo Artist award at the Brit Awards.

When a picture was published the next day of Lily crying into the arms of her boyfriend Seb, a lot of people made the assumption that it she was crying because of her Brits upset and an argument with her friend Amy. However, Lily claimed the tears were a result of the prospect of heading off to another country once again, and leaving Seb alone once more.

The shadow of the Lily–Amy feud lingered on, though. They were two strong women and making fiercely independent music that easily stood head and shoulders with or above that of their male contemporaries. That should have made them the closest of friends. But Amy was like Lily in so many ways; their fierce, aggressive image masked insecurity and self-doubt. So it wasn't surprising that their personalities clashed.

Besides, Amy was never out of the press with her hard-drinking exploits – whether it was for cancelling a gig because of illness hours after she was photographed buying booze, throwing up on stage at London's camp G.A.Y. venue, or getting thrown out of a London hotel for making too much noise.

Compared with Amy, the 'Smile' singer was a wallflower. Lily had done all her hard living in her early teens and had no time for that now – which was a good thing in hindsight, because every time she did have a big night out, she would normally wake up with a huge hangover and some explaining to do to her press team.

The media drooled at the prospect of the two girls slugging it out and slinging headline-worthy insults at each other – and after a slow start they were happy to oblige. Fed up with being constantly questioned about Lily, and annoyed that it had overshadowed her Brits victory, Amy snapped, 'I don't wanna talk about that little prick. I laughed when I saw how fat she'd got.'

Lily hit back at Amy in an interview in America's highly influential magazine *Entertainment Weekly*, fuming, 'she goes to all those parties, though, and hangs out with Kelly Osbourne and Kate Moss. I don't understand that need to become famous. In my country, I think I have a reputation of being a bad role model for kids [and] yet nobody's ever had a picture of me rolling out of a nightclub at five in the morning completely out of my head on Ecstasy and coked out of my brains. I always find that really peculiar. That's never gonna happen to me, because really I'm not like that.

'If I wanted to be, like, a rich and famous celebrity,

I would be going to those celebrity parties and film premieres, but that's just not what I'm here for and not what I find interesting. In my spare time I like to stay at home with my boyfriend and watch television. I have had my days of going out and getting trashed, but I really don't any more.'

It was a fair comment. Unfortunately it couldn't have been made at a worse time as she was soon seen staggering out of a club in Soho on 14 March, very much the worse for wear. An onlooker witnessed the event, saying, 'She decided to walk the mile or so to the Groucho.' On the way there was apparently some commotion with a number of photographers. 'As we were nearing the Groucho, she started posing for pictures. She was laughing one minute, then cussing the next. Her friends had to split up the fight.'

It left Lily a little red-faced. Her spat with Amy seemed a silly thing. It looked as if this was nothing more than a simple misunderstanding that spiralled out of control. It seemed to hinge on the argument that the music world wasn't big enough for two strong-willed girls, which was rubbish. And the pair soon realised that.

At 2007's South by Southwest festival in Austin, Texas, the pair ended their bitter feud. Weeks of animosity were forgotten as the two Brits called it quits while they entertained an American audience. Lily confirmed, 'Me and the Winehouse have made up,' before joking, 'We're now lesbian lovers.' It was good to see, but with both girls displaying the same amount of quick-witted venom whenever they open their mouth, let's hope their feud doesn't flare up again.

Of course, it wasn't Lily's first feud to have turned nasty. We all know that she likes to spout her opinions with a scattergun approach, but most recipients don't bite back. When you're a hardened Australian rocker, though, you tend to stick up for yourself. Lily found that out the hard way when she took on Chris Cester from the rock band Jet.

Chris was born in 1981 in Melbourne, Australia. He and his older brother Nic both became obsessed with their parents' record collection, listening to their Beatles and Rolling Stones albums for hours on end. Both cite *Abbey Road* as their favourite album. They would even put on pretend stadium gigs in their living room together. Chris was always the singer, but he would eventually move to playing drums.

The brothers eventually formed Jet, named after the Paul McCartney song that he sung in the band Wings. Nic would take vocal duties, Chris would play drums, pals Cameron Muncy and Mark Wilson would play guitar and bass respectively. Their iconic hit 'Are You Going To Be My Girl?' was featured on the 2004 worldwide advertising campaign for iPod.

When Lily played the Big Day Out festival in Australia in January, alongside other British acts including Kasabian, the Streets and John Cooper Clark, she got herself into another typical Lily argument. This time it was with Chris Cester. It was at an after-show party and Lily was a little the worse for wear when she found herself getting into the spat. Onlookers claimed it was because Chris had once snubbed her at a Japanese festival. At first, it just seemed to be a drunken outburst drowned out by the loud noise and party-going atmosphere – that was, until Lily called the drummer an arsehole, which prompted Chris to throw a cigarette at her. Enraged, Lily hurled a bottle at his head, which luckily someone caught before it did major damage.

Things then spiralled out of control, with Lily throwing herself at Chris before being dragged off by members of Kasabian. It wouldn't be the first time the British guitar band would be her unlikely saviours. They also came to the rescue when Lily lashed out at Mike Skinner from the Streets during the tour.

Speaking on Australian TV show *Undercover* the

morning after and looking extremely hung-over, she struggled to recollect what had happened the night before.

'I wound Chris the drummer up the wrong way and he flicked a cigarette at me. I then threw a bottle at him which luckily missed and all hell broke loose. I have no recollection of the whole event. I also had a big row with Mike Skinner. I was so drunk I can't even remember what it was about. The Kasabian boys were dragging me off him, saying: "Stop it, Lily! You're being an idiot." They're such a good influence on me.'

Fearing fireworks would spark again the next time Chris and Lily appeared together, organisers moved their trailers away from each other. However, they did make up two weeks later, when they met at Melbourne's Big Day Out after-party and were spotted constantly hugging.

And there was even time for a third attempt at mending some burnt bridges. Just days after making up with Amy, Lily ended another long-term feud with Peaches Geldof. The pair bumped into each other in a London nightclub and, as Peaches explained, 'We looked at each other and thought, "This is rubbish."'

CHAPTER TWENTY-FIVE

LILY POND

'I just do what I'm told. If it goes good, that's great. If not, I'll be home sooner.'

Just as the internet helped Lily break through in her native UK, it has given her a leg up in the lucrative but elusive US market in a new way.

British artists have tried to crack America for as long as pop has dominated the charts – yet few acts have achieved lasting international success. For every Elton John, Rolling Stones and Beatles, there is a Robbie Williams, Oasis and Westlife – mega-successful British acts who have barely managed to touch the surface stateside.

Lily Allen and fellow pop hellraiser Amy

Winehouse look like they have broken the mould. American audiences are sitting up and listening to their music and loving their personalities. Critics are clamouring for tickets to their gigs and reeling out superlatives in their reviews.

While Robbie Williams and Oasis's attitude counted against them in the US, Lily and Amy's individuality is being lapped up. But why? Timing is a key factor – America now seems ready to accept international artists with sass and attitude.

But the presence of an important medium mustn't be ignored. The internet's newest phenomenon – the celebrity blog – must claim a major credit in easing Lily's progress stateside.

Celebrity blogs exploded into public consciousness in the mid-noughties. As broadband internet access has swept across the Western world, so has the thirst for fast and ready-made celebrity news. Very quickly magazines and newspapers have found themselves left behind, with the internet becoming the best source of immediate information.

Blogs rose to the challenge, offering regular daily updates on stars' comings and goings. Often set up by individuals or small groups, they have been heavily laced with opinion, in a way magazines and newspapers could never do. Readers have lapped it up in their millions. And the US-based blogs have been writing about Lily since she first appeared in America in October 2006, to perform at the Troubadour in Los Angeles. They loved what they saw and have been singing her praises ever since.

Thanks to these blogs, Lily's music has been catapulted into millions of American households. This is the kind of exposure money can't buy, and that the artists who tried and failed to break America in the 1980s, 1990s and early 2000s would have killed for.

Lily's biggest supporter stateside is also the gossip-blog generation's biggest success story: Mario Lavandeira, whose perezhilton.com website attracts more than three million hits a day.

Lavandeira jumped on the Lily Allen bandwagon on day one and has remained a fan and keen source of publicity ever since. A fiercely discerning judge of taste and talent, the website mocks, shames and destroys stars on a daily basis. But the few celebrities it backs, it backs all the way. Luckily Lily falls into that camp, and has been a regular fixture on the site since October 2006. Even when she isn't in the US, perezhilton.com has included regular updates of her outbursts, outrageous behaviour and her daily comings and goings, as reported in the British tabloid press.

Perez's postings on Lily include: 'We are thankful for Lily Allen's outspokenness! As if her music weren't fresh enough, her candour in interviews is even more refreshing ... We love us some Lily Allen. Everything about her. She can even pull off the poodle hair!'

The site ran a competition handing out tickets for the singer's US tour and in February 2007 Lavandeira even travelled to London to support her at the Brits, where she was nominated for four prizes. When she walked away empty-handed, he was furious but philosophical: 'Outrage, we say! Outrage! Lily Allen was nominated for four Brit Awards and failed to walk away with any. She wasn't even asked to perform at the ceremony, held Wednesday night in London. The only way to take that is as a personal snub or some vendetta. She wasn't even asked to perform??? Yet Corrine Bailey Ray was???? Bullshit! Better than any Brit award, though, Lily is "making it" in America, achieving that rare crossover success that many UK artists unsuccessfully strive for.'

Perezhilton.com isn't alone in its support of Lily – her movements have been watched and keenly backed by a host of other sites, including thesuperficial.com, defamer.com, TheBosh.com and news blog TMZ.com.

After her Troubadour gig, the Defamer dubbed her 'adorable British musical sensation Lily Allen'.

And TMZ.com reported Allen's appearance at the South by Southwest festival in March 2007, writing, 'British pop star Lily Allen is just beginning to make waves in the States, but she's already got the bloody rock star lifestyle down pat. With her Courtney Love training wheels on, the 21-year-old took the stage with a cigarette and a bottle of beer in hand. Looks likes Lily's music isn't the only thing getting the good buzz!'

Lily's style, sound and all-round individuality have taken America by storm – but it's clear she's had a helping hand from friendly individuals.

A Socialite's Life also waded in with praise, writing, 'Lily Allen is fun. She hates Paris Hilton and wants to punch her in the face. For practice, she kicks the stuffing out of paparazzi. Stay out of her way. British chicks seem way tougher than Americans. We need to import more nasty Cockney chicks here!'

All and all it was a good omen for Lily, and she needed it. Nursing her Brit Awards hangover, she tearfully said goodbye to Seb once again as she headed off to yet another country.

This was the big one, though. Every international

act wants to take a bite at the American market. And Lily was no different. Fears that her music would be too British for the American audience went unheeded as they warmed instantly to the little pop princess. But it would be a gruelling experience for Lily. In America you can receive a lot as a pop star, but you have to put a lot in. And Lily was not the sort of person who could network and be all smiles for the whole day. Question marks were raised as to whether she could handle that kind of demand.

For the moment, though, all Lily cared about that she was missing Seb. Like all young girls in love, she just wanted to be with him and couldn't muster much effort as the prospect of a heavy schedule loomed.

She had tested the water in October 2006, when she played a gig at the Troubadour in LA. And it certainly whetted their appetite, with one journalist dying to hear the album, saying, 'In the U.K. where her debut album *Alright, Still* was released in July, Allen is already a star with two hit singles to her credit. In the U.S., however, that album isn't scheduled for release until January, a curious move, considering the stir Allen has created.'

Instead of issuing it now, her record company were releasing a four-song, digital-only EP. It was a shrewd move that was aimed at capitalising on the hype about Lily that has spread around the web, from MySpace to fans' blogs.

Lily herself bemoaned the fact that her album wouldn't hit the streets for another four months, insisting that she was 'bored of not being famous here'.

What she wasn't bored with was the constant promotion, even on this whistle-stop tour. What fun was to be had revolved around torturing paparazzi. On one occasion she saw a British photographer following her. When she stepped into her limo, she laughed as he frantically hailed a taxi. She told the limo driver to wait until the snapper got in the taxi before losing him in a sea of traffic.

Her Troubadour show had a glittering array of stars in attendance, including Gwen Stefani, Gavin Rossdale, Orlando Bloom and Sean Lennon – who all danced in the balcony as they watched a new star blossom in front of their eyes without showing any signs of wilting in the presence of music and acting royalty. Lennon rightly predicted what everyone was thinking that night. 'She's going to be massive,' he enthused.

But Lily was adamant that she would not change. 'I never went into this to be a role model. These girls see the honesty of me saying, "Yes, I've taken drugs and I drink and I have sex and give my boyfriend blowjobs occasionally." That's just what it's like being my age – and I won't change for America.'

It was a draining trip, but it was a good one as it showed Lily what was expected of her if she wanted to make it there. 'I love London, I love England. I don't think I could move to the States. I like America once I get past customs, but there's something really unwelcoming about it before you get in. And it can be so false. If you had a bad show, it's like, "Oh, my God! You were so fabulous tonight!" But at the same time it's been amazing. I went to the studio the other day and Kanye West was there. He was directing me just because he wanted to. It was too weird.'

When the time came for her to go to America for the main promotional tour she had her doubts. When asked how she thought America would take her she said, 'I don't know, mate. I don't think about it. I just do what I'm told. If it goes good, that's great. If not, I'll be home sooner.'

And she was beginning to suspect that her American label, Capitol Records, weren't all that enthused about her. 'I don't think Capitol Records in America are particularly into the album.'

She did, however, have a cunning ruse to sort that out. She posted the email address of Andy Slater of Capitol Records on her blog and said, 'I've got quite a good plan, if you want my album to be released in America, I suggest you email this man! And if he gets 30,000 emails in the first hour and EMI's servers go down? That'd be good press!'

She need not have worried. The label was putting a lot of effort into making sure Lily would make a successful crossover. The schedule for the first leg of her American promotional tour was as follows. She would appear on the celebrated comedy show *Saturday Night Live* on 3 February and an intimate club tour that kicked off on 5 February in Los Angeles. She would also perform on the famed talk show *Late Night with Conan O'Brien* on 13 February.

Some of Lily's first major press coverage came courtesy of *Interview* magazine. The trendy publication's format was a series of interviews of celebrities by other celebrities. In Lily's case her close family friend and godmother, Angela McCluskey, interviewed her. The Scottish singer was left dazzled at the Lily that now faced her. Gone was the cheeky five-year-old she remembered chasing through country fields; instead the person who stood in front of her was a genuine pop icon. 'Lil's terribly glamorous. It's hard for me to come to terms with the fact this is our Lil,' she said.

Lily revealed the one thing that she loved about

promoting her material in America – no mention of her famous dad. 'I'm excited because there aren't the same kind of class issues in America as there are in Britain – at least as far as I can tell. The thing that gets me down in the UK is that all the questions ask me about my social background and who my father is. In America, no one knows who I am or where I come from, so I'm kind of excited to see what people think without all those kind of prejudgements.'

So far the American tour was going swimmingly. She was an instant hit on *Saturday Night Live*, which was guest-presented by a certain Miss Barrymore. She performed her two biggest tracks 'Smile' and 'LDN' to great effect, proving once and for all she could retain her Britishness without it getting lost in translation.

Cracks began to show almost immediately after the *Saturday Night Live* performance, however. 'This last year has gone so quickly for me. It was only last May that I was playing in London at the Notting Hill Arts Club to 250 people and suddenly I'm in a dressing room right next to Drew Barrymore and Cameron Diaz about to sing on TV to 50 million people or something stupid. Talk about mind fuck. Needless to say I was shitting myself but I think it went OK,' she said.

'I try not to think something like *Saturday Night Live* is a big deal because otherwise my nerves really kick in. But it's kind of difficult when you have a million people running around saying, "You should be really happy you're doing this." It's like, "Yeah, maybe I would be if I'd wanted to be a huge international superstar my whole life" … but I don't!'

After the show her mum and Seb visited her. It was an emotional reunion. 'I spent an hour crying on the floor of the Soho Grand Hotel lobby saying goodbye to them before getting on another plane to LA. It felt like going back to school after the holidays, if that makes sense. I don't know when I'm going to see them again.'

A few weeks later she was pining for her boyfriend so much she contemplated her choices: 'I'm on a US tour till May. Or I could go home to my fella, then write a new album.' However, cancelling 14 tour dates was never a really viable option. But Lily was even starting to tire of her hit single 'Smile'. 'I'm not sick of playing it, but it's really hard to be enthused about it … It's difficult to be energetic about it, because I've probably sang it 2,000 times.'

Next up was the celebrated Texan music festival South by Southwest in March. The festival's creative director, Brent Grulke, was hoping she'd make the crossover. 'She's very distinctive, and it's the kind of thing where there aren't a lot of antecedents that would be applicable for US success. Can she have a career in the US? That's an intellectually interesting question to me. And I also am quite certain that particularly young women view her as powerful and as someone who's in control of her destiny.'

She immediately made her mark at the festival. 'It's all very weird here. They're all backward in Texas but not as much as they are in Arkansas and Wyoming where I'm going soon. I can't really speak for the American population – I'm so far away from anything they are and stand for.'

Fearing a backlash from this extremely patriotic nation, she immediately apologised, claiming her comments were fuelled by alcohol. 'Apparently I said that all Americans are backwards in some interview. While some Americans probably are – every country has a backwards contingent – that would be a sweeping generalisation and also not true. I think there are some very clever Americans. I don't actually remember saying these things, but they were said in Texas which is where the South by Southwest festival was, therefore I must have been very drunk and showing off.'

It wasn't the first time she would be apologising at

the festival. Once again she had to suffer taunts from critics after she turned up to a show drunk just weeks after slamming Amy Winehouse for her partying ways.

Lily performed a lacklustre late show in Austin on 14 March which started with her staggering onstage with a bottle of beer and a cigarette, apologising to fans for being drunk 'because it's 11 o'clock'.

While she drunkenly performed on stage, she couldn't resist another dig at her old rivals the *NME*, who were the Texas show's co-promoter: 'Everyone from the *NME* can fuck off!' And she picked on one reporter at the show, giggling that he had 'the smallest penis ever seen'. She ended her show reminding the sold-out 1,500-capacity crowd, 'I just want to say once again how much I hate *NME*.'

It's still early days in Lily's bid to conquer the world's biggest music industry but the omens look good. She stands out as a breath of fresh air and America has always preferred our acts to wear their nationality on their sleeve rather than pretend they are something they are not. And Lily has no problem with that.

CHAPTER TWENTY-SIX

ONWARDS AND UPWARDS

'I feel like I've dealt with a lot of emotional shit that people don't normally deal with until their twenties or thirties and I'm already on my way to figuring out happiness.'

With a multi-platinum-selling album, a handful of hit singles and a clutch of awards to her name, 2007 was Lily's year. But while her career saw her catapulted into the limelight, her love life was heading in the opposite direction and in August, Lily split from her longtime boyfriend Seb Chew. Although Lily had become a tabloid darling, she managed to keep her break-up with Seb relatively low-key. It was only when she declared herself single at the *GQ* Awards in September that the world was alerted to her heartbreak: 'Seb and I aren't together any more. I split with him a month ago so I'm single now.'

But despite her status as one of Britain's hottest young stars, Lily continued to battle with insecurities about her looks and the end of her two-and-a-half year relationship with Seb seemed to exacerbate them. She hit the party scene hard in an effort to forget her problems, but her wild and drunken nights out often did little to soothe her body hang-ups. 'I always think that no one is ever going to fancy me. Part of the reason I came out tonight is because I'm back on the market and I need to get in practice. I don't know if I can pull any more,' she said one evening. 'I'm enjoying being back here in London. I just hope I can find a new boyfriend.'

Lily needn't have worried, though, as a few weeks later she met The Chemical Brothers' Ed Simons and the pair hit it off immediately. They began dating in September and the effect the new romance had on Lily's outlook on life was noticeable. She also addressed the hectic schedule typical of the previous twelve months, not to mention the family strife, dognapping, fighting with friends and award losses, working out and revising her diet of fatty foods to reflect a new, more health-conscious Lily. And thanks to her new fitness regime, coupled with a bout of hypnotherapy, she lost two stone in just over a month and dropped from a size 12 to a size 8.

'I looked awful a few months ago. I used to stuff my face with pies because I was depressed. But I'm chuffed that I've lost weight already. I'm going to the gym two to three nights a week. And I've swapped junk food for healthy fruit breakfasts.'

While many credited her health kick and slimmed down figure to her reinvigorated love life, we would later discover her weight loss was on the advice of her doctor, who had diagnosed her with a heart murmur.

Health issues aside, Lily's personal life was looking up and she went public with her romance with 37-year-old Ed in October. In fact, Lily's blossoming relationship put her so at ease with herself, she no longer needed to attend therapy sessions – sessions which had allowed her 'to vent' about the deeply-buried angst she'd carried with her since she was a young teen.

'[My counsellor] was like, "Right, you don't need to come any more. Frankly, it's a waste of your money. You're happy." I've never felt like this before in my entire life. I actually don't have one bad thing to say about anything.'

The couple was fiercely private about their love

for one another, and although they had no qualms about being pictured together out and about on the streets of London, they spoke little about their relationship in the press and never once attended showbiz events as a couple. But the reason for this appeared to lie more with Ed's unease with the press than anything else.

When asked about her new man, Lily would only admit: 'I'm not saying I'm in love. He'll go mad. I'm in like... We really like each other.'

That 'like' would quickly develop into love and it became clear their romance was serious when, within two months of dating, Lily splashed out £700,000 on a new mansion in north London with a view to moving her boyfriend in. After purchasing the property in November, she said, 'I'm moving there in January. Ed and I haven't discussed when he'll move in yet, but we both know it will happen.'

With her personal life ticking along nicely, Lily was in the mood to branch out into new fields – as demonstrated by her decision to accept the offer to become a judge on the panel of the Orange Broadband Prize For Fiction, one of Britain's most prestigious literary awards for female authors, whose previous winners include novelists Zadie Smith and Lionel Shriver. Lily soon discovered that in order to do the role justice, she would have to dedicate many hours to book reading.

'I decided to take up the offer of being one of the judges for The Orange Book Prize for Fiction, I have three more books to finish by the end of the week, having read roughly 20 already.' However, fears over deadlines to read books and other such trivial matters were consigned to the background when it was revealed Lily was expecting a baby with Ed.

News of Lily's pregnancy spread like wildfire and once again the spotlight was turned onto the happy couple. In a statement released just hours after the baby news hit the headlines, Lily's representative said they were 'obviously both thrilled by the news'. The spokesperson added: 'As the pregnancy is at a very, very early stage, the couple ask that you respect their privacy, as the health of Lily and their child is their paramount concern.'

The child would be the first for both Lily and Ed, but neither would have imagined starting a family so soon into their relationship. Lily admitted that much herself during a magazine interview with *Marie Claire* just weeks before she discovered she was pregnant: 'If I was in the right relationship, I'd like to have a child in about two or three years' time.'

Yet, perhaps because of her family background,

Lily has long held thoughts of becoming a mother – having spent the last eight years gathering furniture and keepsakes for the house she would eventually call her home. 'I've been collecting stuff for my house since I was about 14 years old: Moroccan rugs, Eames chairs, lithographs, French farmhouse tables. I think it's quite telling that even though I've never had a house, I've been building a nest since I was 14.'

And while Lily often comes across as a headstrong, independent sort of woman, she has confessed she would like nothing more than to settle down and become a traditional housewife.

'I've looked forward to being stable my whole life. My parents are amazing, but it has been a whirlwind upbringing. I definitely have got my eye on the prize, which is having kids and getting married and cooking dinner and doing homework with my children.'

However ecstatic Lily was at having a baby, her news would attract criticism from other parents and child welfare groups, who feared she was setting the wrong example for her young fans. Lily was more than aware of the controversy her situation would cause, especially because of her recent comments regarding teen pregnancies. 'People are having kids too young and nothing is being done about it,' she had moaned.

But she was quick to dispel any notions about

cashing in on her bulging belly to launch a clothing range for mums-to-be for high street store New Look, insisting she didn't want to encourage other youngsters to follow her lead: 'I've had a lot of offers from people to do my own maternity range but I don't think it is the right message to send to young Britain. I'm not the best example. I'm pregnant and a bit young, aren't I? My demographic is generally young girls. I don't think a maternity line is particularly suitable.'

Although Lily evidently cares about the wellbeing of her young fans, she has always insisted it is not her duty in life to be a role model: 'I don't see myself as a role model; people should look to mothers and sisters for role models.'

The baby was due to be born in early summer 2008 – around the same time her record label had expected to release her sophomore album. But the timescale was tentative and with Lily resting up instead of heading back into the studio, it looked likely any plans for a release would now be postponed until the end of the year.

Her BBC Three talkshow *Lily Allen and Friends* was also due to start filming in the new year, but Lily was adamant she would honour her commitments to the programme as scheduled. Blogging about her pregnancy for the first time, she wrote: 'As you might already know, the BBC have been silly enough to fund my very own TV show. It will be on in the new year on BBC Three and I am very excited about it. There will be good celebrity guests, not rubbish ones and brilliant bands playing brilliant music. And of course a pregnant me trying to present it all.'

Being an expectant mum gave Lily a whole new purpose in life and she set about making changes to her daily routine. She returned to hypnotherapist Susan Hepburn to help her quit smoking and soon enough managed to kick her 20-a-day habit. She was also more conscious about her alcohol intake and became noticeably absent from the club circuit over the festive period, opting instead for cosy nights in with Ed.

And cheeky Lily made the most of her pregnancy to get her friends and family to attend to her every need. 'She's at home in bed and everyone is running around after her,' said her brother Alfie. 'Mind you, you have to look after Lily even if she isn't pregnant.'

But Lily and Ed's delight at becoming prospective parents would soon diminish, after a romantic New Years' holiday to the Maldives ended in tragedy. Lily had just entered her second trimester when she learned she had suffered a miscarriage.

The couple had barely touched down on British soil when their devastating news was splashed across the tabloids. Faced with the heartbreaking reality, the couple holed themselves up indoors and tried to deal with their sadness together, away from the glare of the media.

They acknowledged their loss in a curt statement to the press, but refused to comment further. The statement, made via her record label spokesman, read: 'We can confirm that Lily Allen has suffered a miscarriage... and we ask that their privacy be respected during this difficult time.'

Almost as soon as the news surfaced, Lily's MySpace page was flooded with messages of support and condolences, and it must have provided some comfort for her to know that so many people were rooting for her. The couple put on a united front when they finally ventured out of their home after a week of self-reflection, embarking on a shopping trip that would put a smile on any girl's face – to the BMW showroom.

Lily purchased a £36,000 convertible but it was obvious even a sports car of such high calibre would do little to heal the massive void she had been left with. It was, however, a testing time for their romance and despite their best efforts, a fortnight after announcing the loss of their baby, Lily found herself single again, seemingly back at square one in the relationship stakes. Her whirlwind romance with Ed had become somewhat of a fantasy in the months leading up to the New Year, but by February her world had come crashing down around her.

Lily's attempts to bounce back saw her returning to her favourite haunts, relying on her nicotine addiction and late-night partying to get her through the stress of it all. And in her first blog since her baby tragedy and break-up, Lily admitted the only thing that had lifted her spirits of late was a spot of retail therapy: 'I have been miserable lately so I bought myself a new car. It may arrive by the end of the week so something to look forward to. Life is funny isn't it? To think that a MacBook or a car is going to be the thing to make you feel better. Something will, soon I hope.'

Lily may have been feeling down in the dumps, but reports persistently suggested a reconciliation with Ed was on the cards. She was spotted wearing an engagement ring at the London premiere of Scarlett Johansson's movie *The Other Boleyn Girl* in February 2008 and further fuelled rumours of a reunion after she was seen leaving Ed's London home.

Then again, she appeared to be scouting around for a new man after unveiling a secret crush on an unlikely candidate – comedian Ricky Gervais: 'Ricky's my type. I quite like the older man. Has he got a hairy back? I like men with a bit of meat and a bit of hair. Not on the head though, I prefer them bald.'

Despite a traumatic couple of months, Lily managed to pick herself up to witness her brother Alfie's debut performance in stage play *Equus* – although she did turn up 10 minutes late, causing her to miss his opening scenes. Not that Alfie would have minded: he received a standing ovation for his critically-acclaimed performance at the Festival Theatre in Chichester, and no one clapped more enthusiastically than proud dad Keith and sister Lily. Frankly, he deserved it for the bravery it must have taken to strip nude on stage, if not for his acting prowess.

But while Alfie was enjoying his spell in the limelight, Lily's career hit a rocky patch. Having been named as the face of upmarket lingerie firm Agent Provocateur in November 2007, Lily's contract with the company was suddenly terminated in February 2008 as the result of a reported rift between bosses Joe Corre and Serena Rees, who were in the midst of a divorce.

To confound matters, poor Lily was then left £3,500 out of pocket after a stripper stole her account details for a local taxi company and used the service on the singer's expense. Lily only realised the fraud was taking place after she was sent the huge bill through the post. 'One of my biggest luxuries in life is taking cabs. Then I found out a stripper had stolen my details and run up a £3,500 bill! She was using my taxi firm to drop her off for work at her strip club every night – and charging me.'

Lily couldn't even cheer herself up with a ticket to the Spice Girls reunion: 'I was told I'd been blacklisted and wasn't allowed a ticket. I still have no idea why.' What should have propelled her back to happiness – in her professional life, at least – was the prospect of her eagerly-awaited TV show. Unfortunately, *Lily Allen and Friends* didn't start with the hoped-for bang, just two days after revealing the heartbreak of her miscarriage. Over 150 fans selected from Lily's friends on MySpace attended the taping at Pinewood Studios in Buckinghamshire and watched as she struggled to read handwritten cue cards after a teleprompter broke. The following day, the *Mail On Sunday* reported that a third of the audience walked out complaining of boredom.

According to the newspaper, one uncomfortable audience member commented: 'Everyone really, really wanted it to work for Lily. She is such a lovely person but all the jokes fell flat and she seemed very nervous. It just did not work. I do think she's got a nice voice but she didn't sing at all. I think everyone was expecting she would.'

Lily was quick to quash the negative reports, insisting the studio audience only left halfway through the show because recording over-ran. 'My TV show recording went really well on Friday. I was s**tting it but I'm really happy with the results and the audience were great. Standing in a hot studio for two hours watching me fluff my lines is not my idea of fun, but they seemed to enjoy it.'

And, not one to simply turn a blind eye to bad press, Lily then took a swipe at the Sunday tabloid: 'Thank you to the ever supportive *Mail On Sunday* for their glittering and rave review of the recording. They insinuated a third of the audience left because they were bored of the content of the show when in fact, due to it being the first show we've done, we ran over a little and naturally a small number of the audience had to catch the last trains back to wherever they came from. I can't imagine the "undercover journalist" who broke into the studio ever had the intention of being positive about it though, obviously.'

In fact, Lily has always had a frosty relationship with the press, and made her feelings for tabloid newspapers crystal clear long before they turned on her chat show: 'If I don't see them, they don't exist.'

Despite Lily's attempts to defend her show against what she claimed to be fabricated reports, the show's future was thrown into further doubt when the debut programme only managed to pull in a small TV-viewing audience. According to official figures, the show's debut episode attracted a mere 255,000 viewers, which equates to just two per cent of the potential audience. A BBC Three spokesman called it a 'solid start' but the news fuelled speculation the programme would not be commissioned for a second series.

Whether or not she makes it as a TV personality remains to be seen, but one thing Lily can depend on is the one reason she became a household name in the first place, her music. However, even this has become the subject of scrutiny. Well, for Natasha Bedingfield at least. Speaking from the United States, the singer urged Lily to ditch the strong London accent she incorporates into her singing voice: 'When I was in England last year it was all about girls with Cockney accents – Lily Allen and Kate Nash. It's all inspired by people like The Streets and Dizzee Rascal. I liked it but I'll be happy when normal voices come back.'

Then Blur frontman Damon Albarn scrapped plans to duet with her, insisting they were musically incompatible. Damon realised this soon into their short-lived collaboration when his unconventional take on music appeared to offend Lily's ears. He said: 'The record label thought it would be a good idea. She came down to my studio and said normally she would just sit around and listen to a musician and come up with some ideas. I jumped on the piano and played some mad stuff and she just looked at me – it didn't exactly go well. She's a really talented kid but it was a bad idea.'

For some unknown reason, Lily also cut contact with music's man-of-the-moment Mark Ronson, although the producer was quick to abolish rumours the pair had fallen out: 'Lily hasn't fallen out with me but I called her and she didn't call back. I've not spoken to her for a while.'

By February, Lily was back on the party scene with a vengeance and her nights out were well documented in the papers. However, she grew rapidly frustrated with journalists' infatuation with celebrity women who like a drink or two and slammed tabloids for their sexist attitudes, accusing them of focusing on the drunken antics of female stars and ignoring those of their male counterparts: 'I don't think [the tabloids] like young women doing well, or having fun. I mean, James Blunt goes out and gets on it and no one cares. We do that and it's all over the papers. It's sad. Those people who write for those gossip magazines, they're not even writers. They can't even punctuate.'

Perhaps Lily's criticism of some journalists' poor grammar came after spending time ploughing through the Orange longlist. However, towards the end of March, there were reports that she had been too depressed to attend a meeting with her fellow judges, and in mid-April, Kirsty Lang, chairman of the panel, confirmed that Lily was no longer involved. Defending the controversial involvement in such a highbrow prize, Lang described how 'Life got in the way' for Lily to keep to her commitments, and lambasted critics for being 'snobby and elitist.'

'She lost a baby, her boyfriend left her and she was launching a new TV show. She was under a hell of a lot of pressure,' she told the *Times*, adding, 'She reads, she writes her own songs. She's a wordsmith.'

As keen as newspapers are to write up damning or

glowing critiques of her career moves, they're equally – if not more – concerned with any movements in her personal life. And speculation over the men in Lily's life has continued unabated. Of course, if you're single, sexy and you're in the public eye, the press will have you dating someone new every day of the week.

Apart from rumours of a reunion with Ed and her self-confessed crush on Ricky Gervais, Lily has been linked with a series of men since her split from the Chemical Brothers star. According to sources, Lily struck up a close friendship with Harry Potter actor Rupert Grint before she started dating Ed. And reports suggest she's rekindled her interest in Rupert, who has played a major role in guiding her through the aftermath of her miscarriage and split from Ed. A source said: 'They swapped numbers then and although they texted each other quite regularly they didn't meet up. Then when Lily split from Ed, Rupert offered her a shoulder to cry on and she took it. They get on really well and he makes her laugh. Last week they enjoyed a Japanese meal together where they had a long intense talk as well as a few laughs.'

Then again, it's not inconceivable for a man and a woman to be just good friends, which may explain why Lily was snapped taking ex-boyfriend Seb Chew to The Ivy for a swanky meal. Once again, the media had a field day theorising that Lily had returned to her first love, but no sooner had the ink dried on the gossip pages, was she seen being escorted home from a charity gig with actor and BAFTA winner James Corden, whom she met on her chatshow.

Whatever may happen in the future, there is no doubt Lily has made a substantial impact on music history. Armed with a handful of songs and a keen eye, her debut album brimmed with originality and innovation. In little more than eighteen months she set a template which many aspiring pop stars quickly latched on to. She has done what every middle child in a family longs to – stand out. As multi-award-winning producer Mark Ronson puts it: 'I think Lily Allen is the greatest melody writer of her generation.' As glowing endorsements go, this is surely one Lily can read repeatedly whenever she's having a down day in LDN.